# The Horrors

a coloring book for adults.

Copyright 2013, 2018 Anji Marth, all rights reserved.

This book is for Michelle, Deb and Bruki.

Welcome to edition three of The Horrors. First self-published, then picked up by a publisher, and now self-published again, this book has been the work of many hours and lots of love. This edition includes the Sheila-na-gig, censored by the publisher in the second edition, as well as the original monsters from both edition one and two, and a few new creatures.

Reminder: this book is intended for adults, since it's got violence, gore, and sexuality in it.

It's my pleasure to provide you with all the reasons behind the things that go bump in the night, once again.

~Anji Marth 2018

Since the beginning of time, tales of cryptids, ghosts, and monsters have been used to explain our fears. Generally the fear comes first, best described as the darkness around the primordial fire, one full of hungry eyes. Then there are the sound and sensory experiences; from the eaves whistling in the wind at midnight, to the creak of a staircase when nobody is there, to the cold drafts we feel at the most unexpected moments.

Thankfully there's an explanation. The wind frightens us because it sometimes sounds like a human voice, calling out in hunger and desperation. The darkness becomes unsettling, as it may contain monsters which will devour or change us. The deep sea is an endless mystery, extending far below our paddling feet.

Are THE HORRORS real? I've encountered a few of the creatures in this tattoo coloring book. There's a good chance you may have as well; maybe your brother did, or a friend of a friend. Urban legends and myths are things we rarely come into personal contact with, but stories we hear over and over again. These stories are often intended to correct our bad, sometimes dangerous, behaviors and impulses. Many of these creatures appear as punishment for misdeeds; some appear when one violates a certain taboo. Others will reveal themselves when we enter their sacred ground.
Maybe we tell these stories to control ourselves. Maybe we tell them because we like to feel afraid.
I know I like to feel afraid. I hope these creatures frighten you as much as they frightened me while drawing them.

~2013

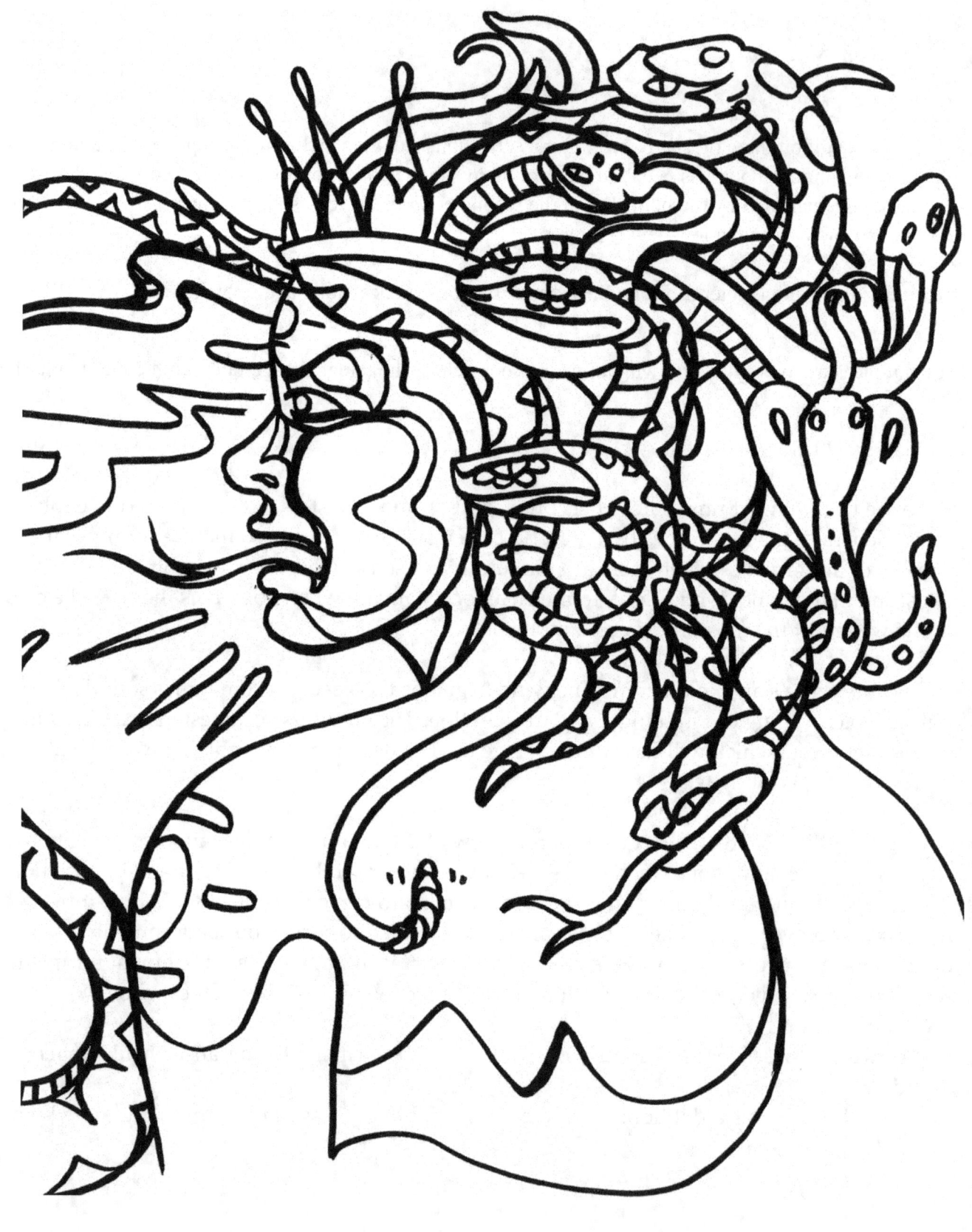

# Gorgon

The gorgons are deformed women who've been punished by the gods, in Greek myth and legend. The most famous Gorgon, of course, is Medusa- who was punished for her vanity by being given an appearance so hideous that a look at her would turn a man to stone.

With the upper body of a woman and hair made of snakes, she lived a solitary existence, except those few warriors who showed up, trying to kill her.

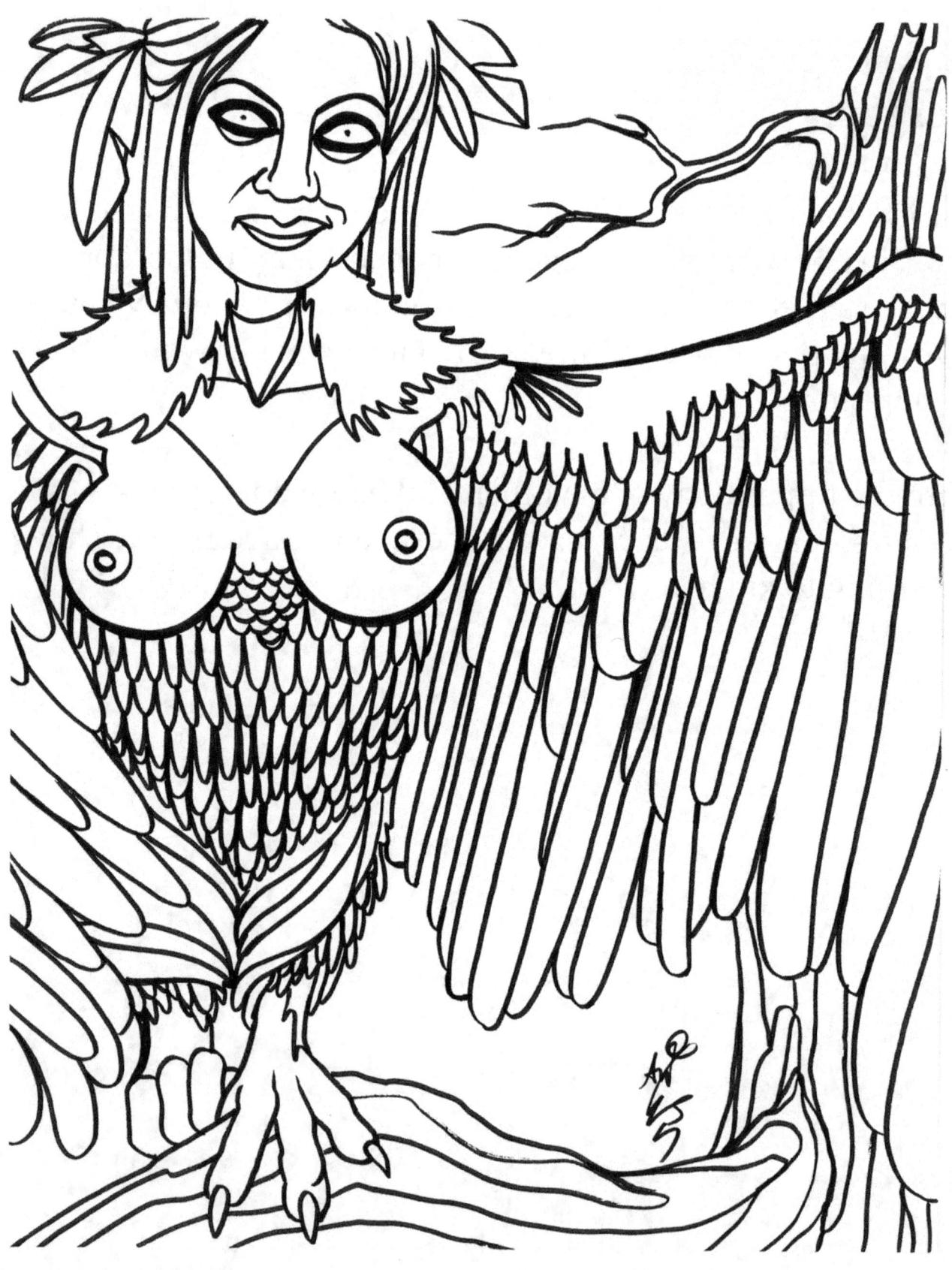

# Harpy

Harpies originate in Greek and Russian mythology. They're women who inhabit the bodies of predatory or scavenging birds, who can foretell the future. In Russia they are called "Alkonost" and are only seen when delivering an important message.

They are known to steal food from camps, and to carry away evildoers, as well as occasional the well-fed child. They arrive with a great whipping of the wind.

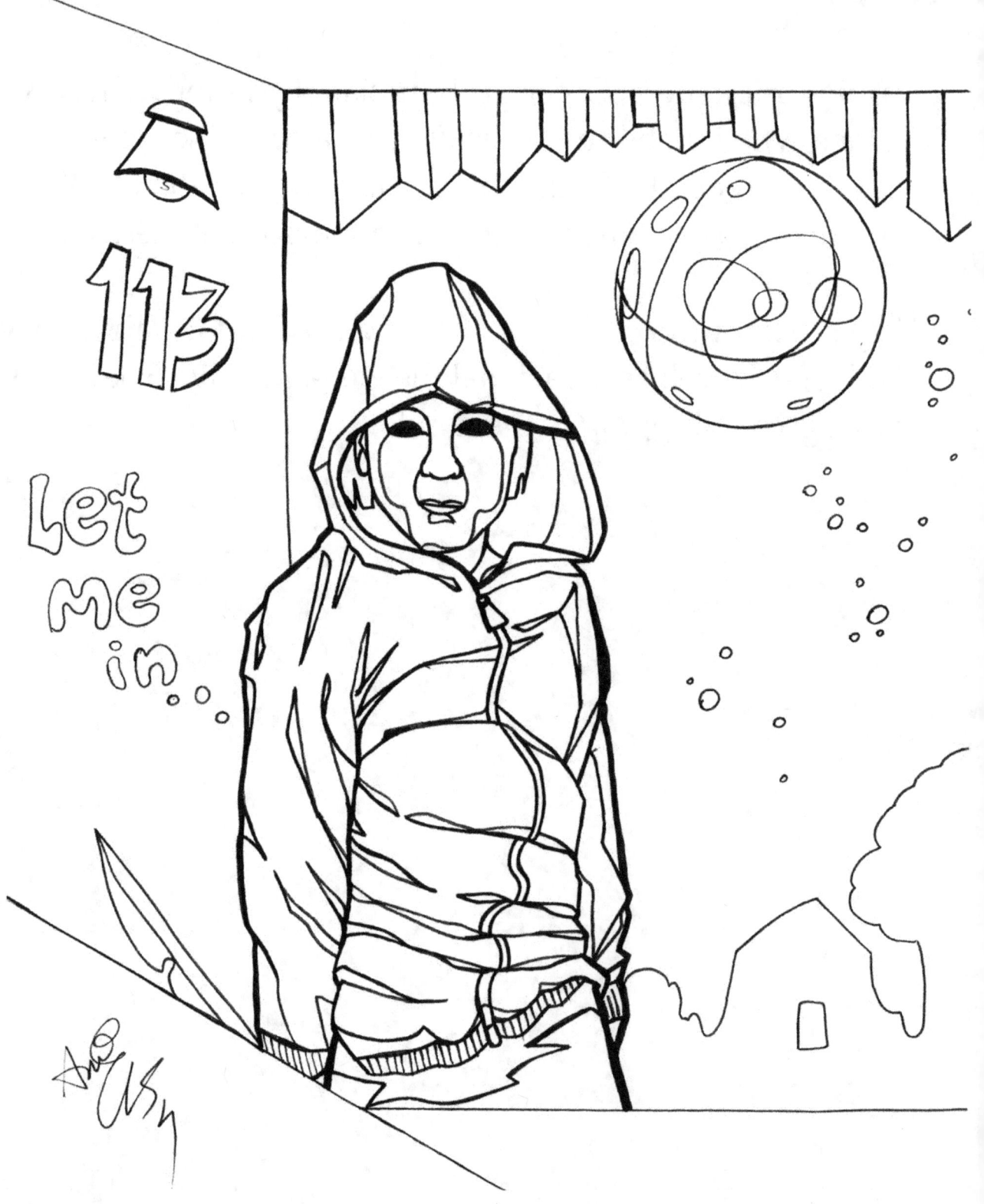

# Black-eyed kids

The BEK are a modern urban legend, which began with a few sightings and reports. They have since been sighted all over the world and in all kinds of situations.

Usually, one or two BEK will be found together. They look completely normal, like older children or very young teens, dressed in modern clothing. They will knock on a door and ask to use the phone or to get a drink of water. If they are on the road, they will tap on car windows and ask for a ride.

Usually people report feeling ill or confused in their presence. They will persist in demanding entry to the house or car, until and unless the person finally notices that their eyes are completely black (having no white sclera). At this point, they will go away, leaving the person exhausted or full of vague dread.

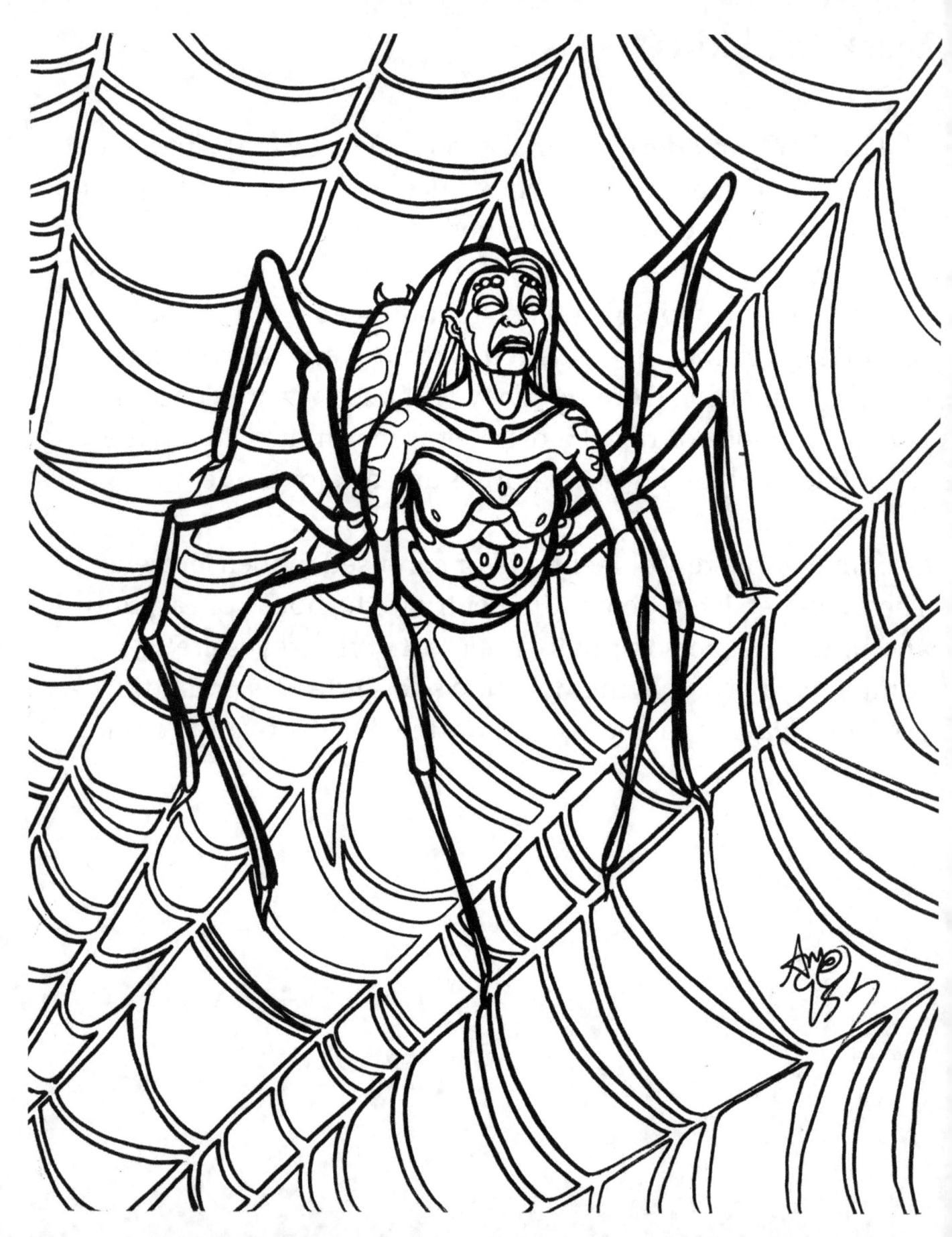

# Jorogumo

In Japanese this creature is literally known as "whore spider." This creature is one of the Yokai, traditional monsters in local folklore and legend. Modern reports of these creatures state that they live in apartments or rooms that are covered in sticky webbing, and that they may be able to appear nearly human.

They will go out and attract men back to their rooms, then use poison to sedate them, feeding on their prey for weeks. When the victim dies, they discard the husk and go out hunting again.

When in the guise of a human, they appear as young women and rarely speak. Once they shed their human disguise, they are massive spiders with a woman's upper body attached. They are as intelligent as human beings.

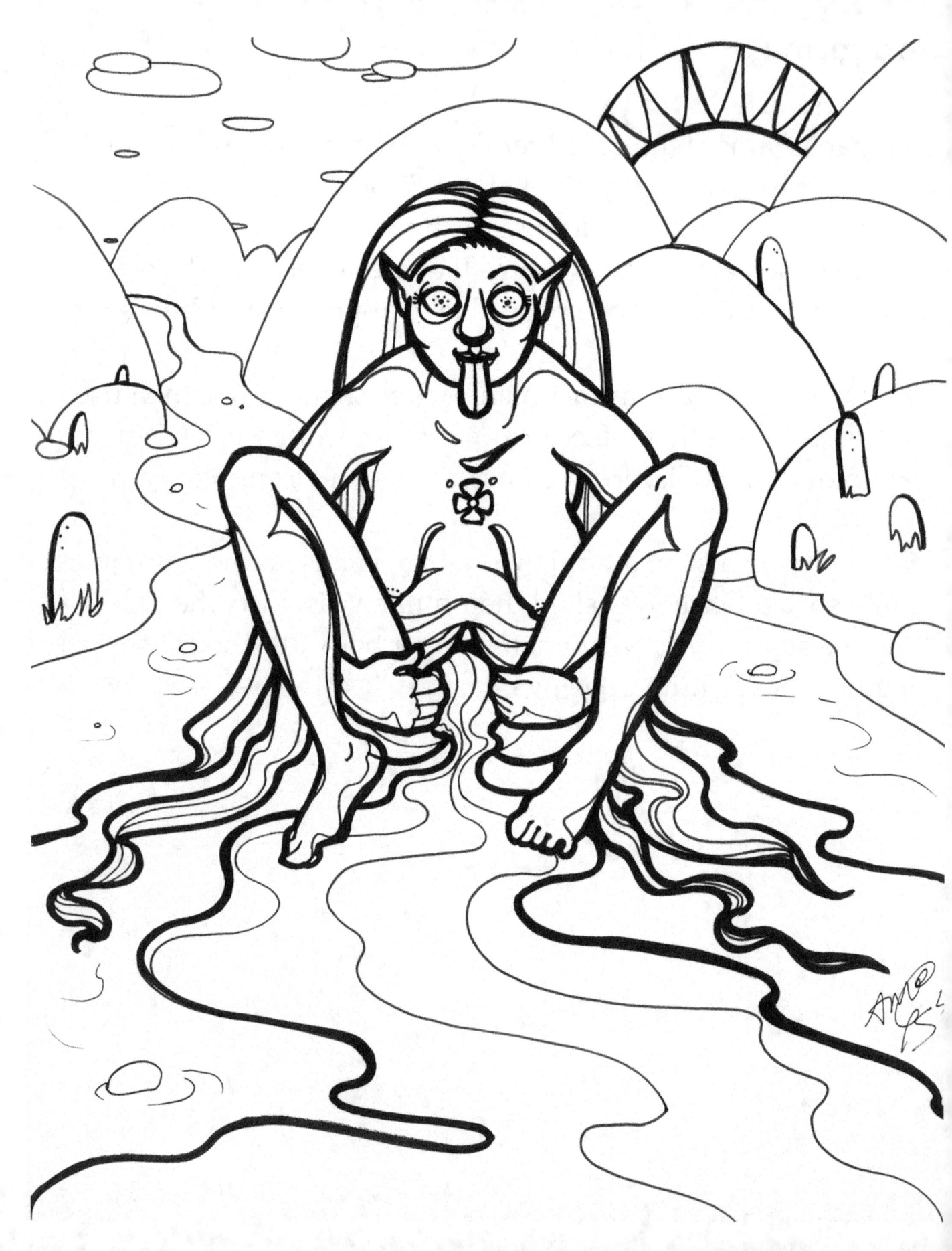

# Sheila na gig

The Sheila na gig is an Irish legend that has been carved on ancient buildings and into rocks there since archaic times. A woman holding open her vagina, with either blood, water, or leaves pouring forth; she's a well-known figure in myth.

She is meant to represent fertility, but there is also a myth that a Sheila na gig is a forest spirit. It's believed that any spring in the woods is in fact her open vagina; that the waters found in springs like this are intoxicating in some way and will make its drinker confused or disoriented.

Like most Irish myths, her intoxication can cause a person to lose time, to become lost forever or to age rapidly.

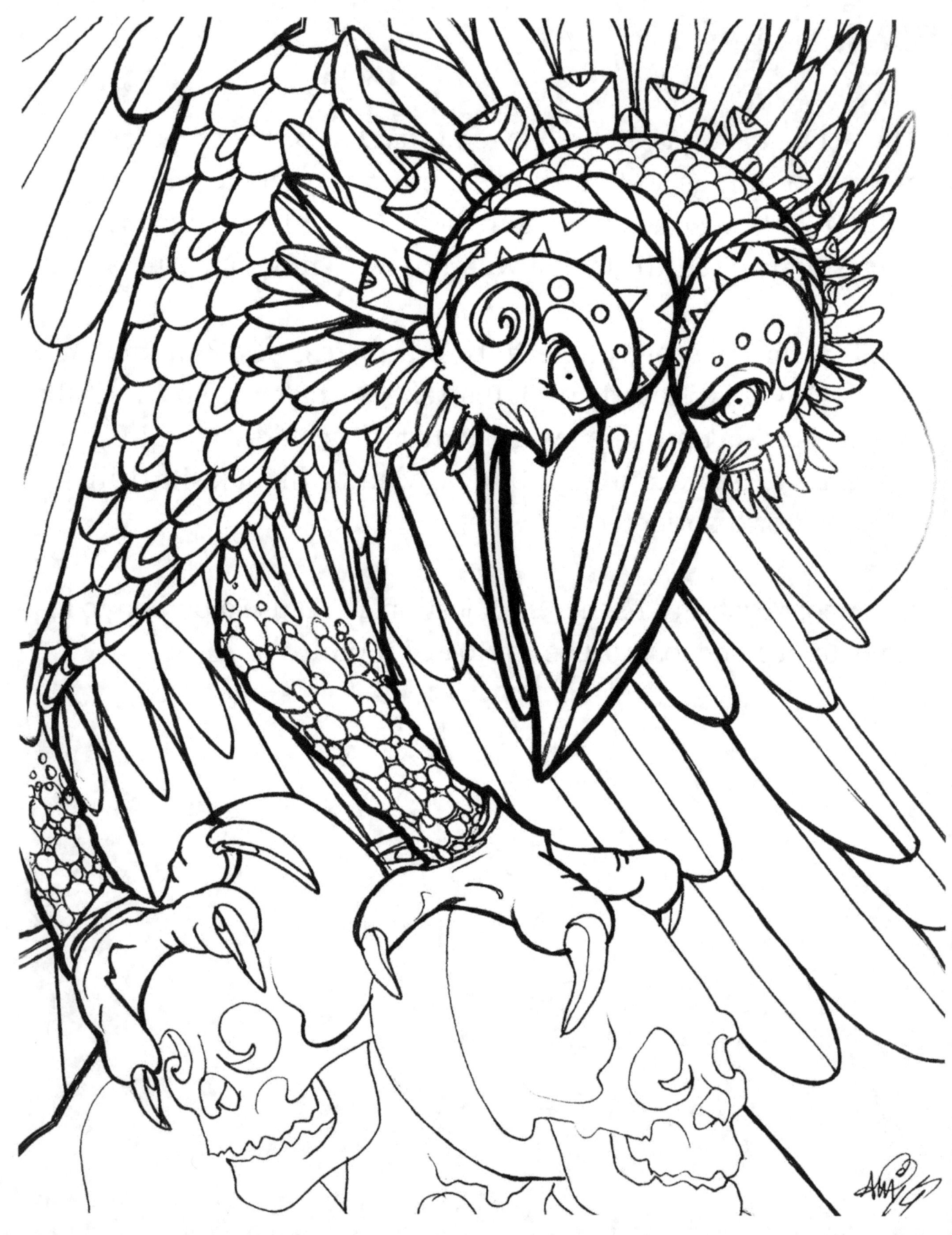

# Thunderbird

The native tribes of the Pacific Northwest said that the Thunderbird came with large storms, and that its flight caused lightning. The Thunderbird is a common myth among many Native American peoples, although descriptions vary. Common traits include a massive size, a voice as loud as thunder, and a diet of humans or large land animals. It is considered supernatural, paranormal, and not an actual animal.

It's agreed that staying out of the Thunderbird's way is the best course of action; no means of stopping it or killing it are known. Cowichan tribes believed that the Thunderbird could shapeshift into human form, and even marry into human families. Despite its supernatural and historical origin, the Thunderbird is also a cryptozoological mystery. There have been numerous sightings of a "big bird" flying low over cars and camps in the American Southwest and in South America, as well reports and photographs of giant birds being shot down or captured.

Some claim it may be pterodactyls or similar animals that have somehow survived for eons, without being seen or caught. Others believe it to be a new species, unknown to science. The Thunderbird exists in native lore from Alaska to Argentina; modern sightings span the same area. This giant bird is an old myth, as well as a new mystery.

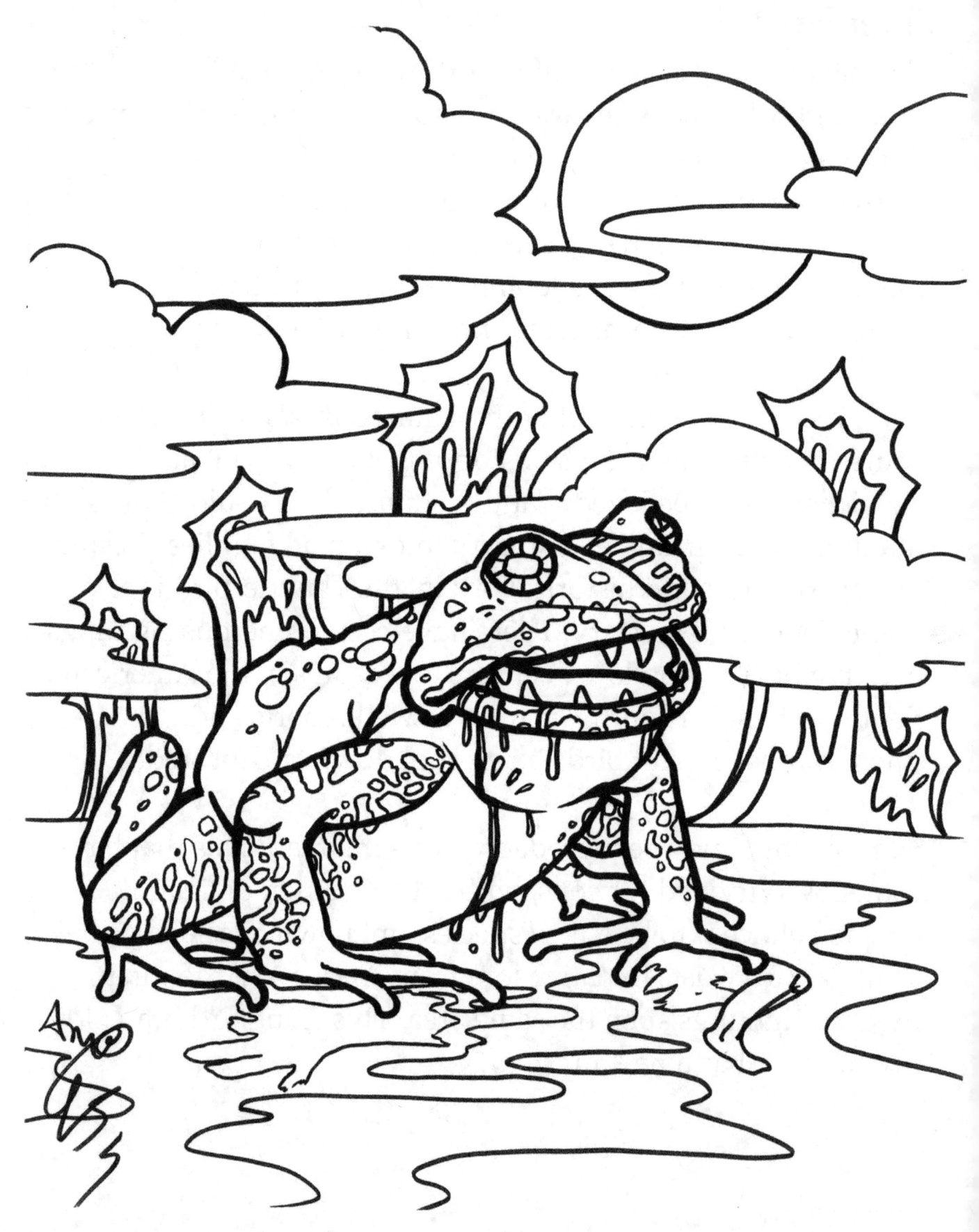

# Wuhnan Toads

These are giant albino toads that live in a lake in China in the Hubei Province. They have an appetite to match their size.

They are larger than full-grown oxen, eating anything that crosses their path. They are reported to come out of the lake at dusk and eat humans, livestock, and any wild animals they can find, then retreat to the water at daylight.

They're most often sighted by fishermen, who see them leaving or returning to the lake.

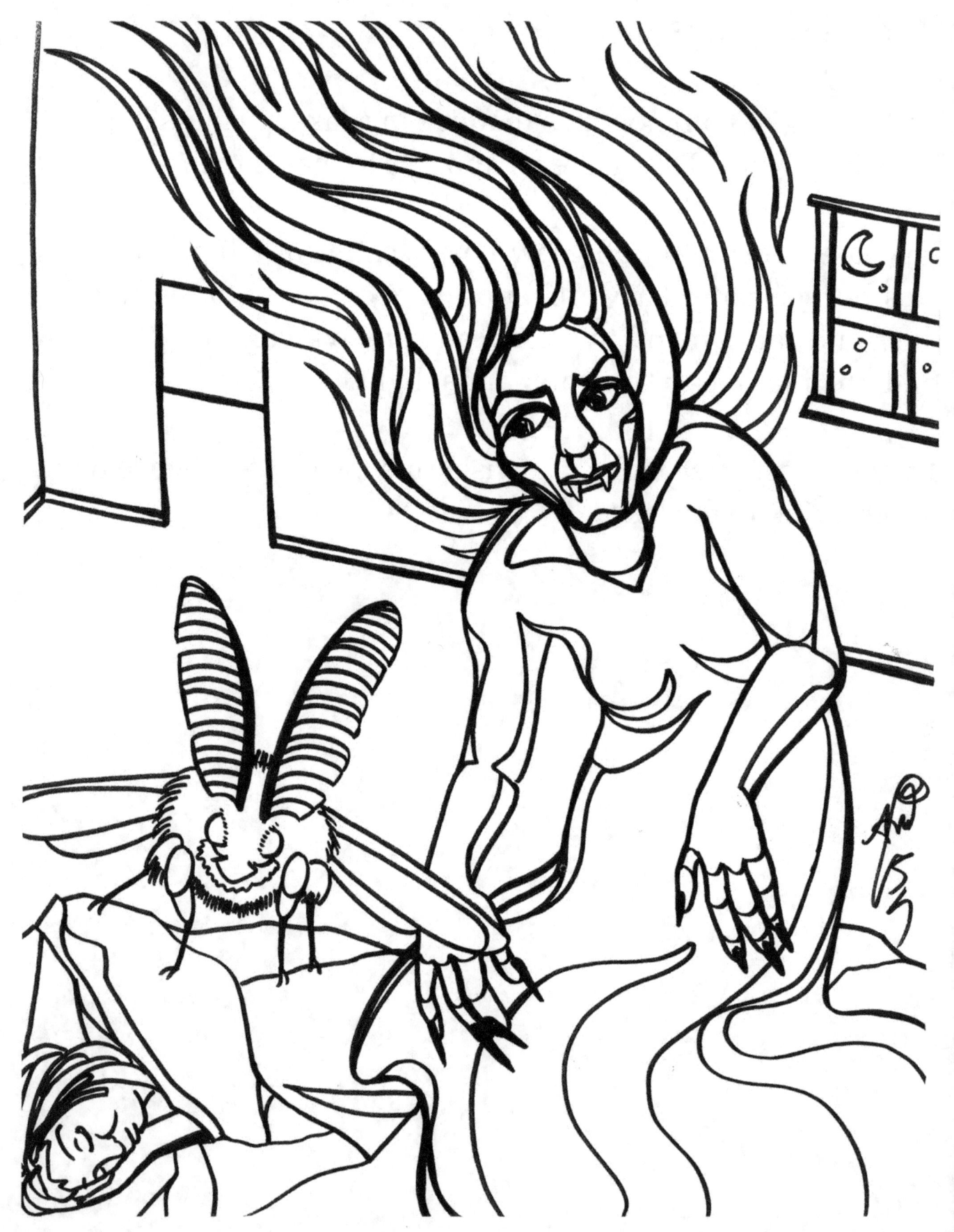

# Mara/Nocnista

The Mara, or Nocnista in Polish, is a night-hag which creates nightmares and feeds on fear. The Nocnista can change form, becoming a moth or a wisp of hair that the victim may accidentally breathe in.

The Mara sneak into bedrooms at night and crush the chests of sleepers, resulting in terrifying dreams. They are also known to torment horses, riding them all night until they die or are exhausted in the morning.

The best way to defend against them is to keep iron nearby, as iron is a natural repellent. There is a belief that iron bedsteads may have been created originally to keep the Nocnista at bay.

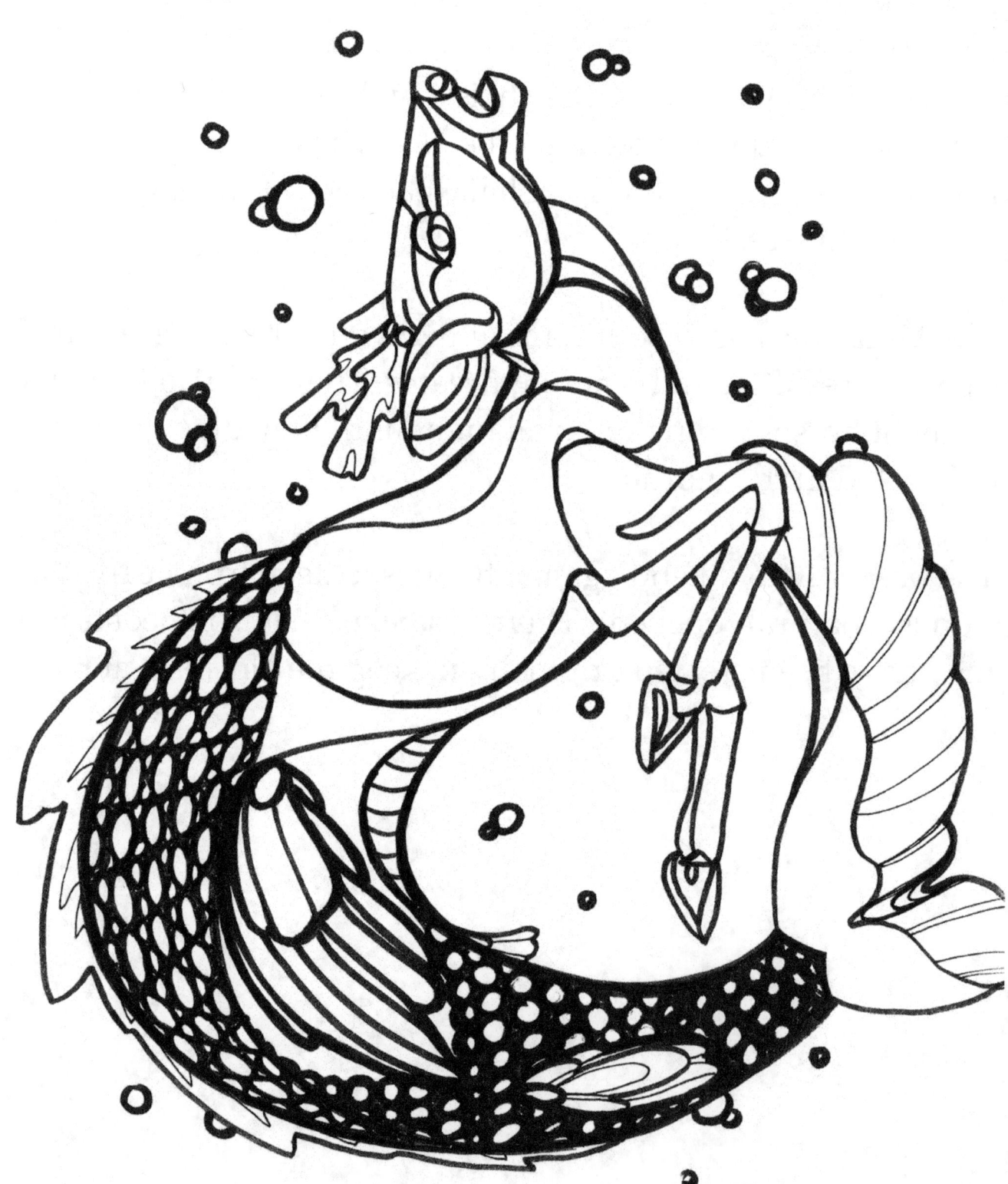

# Makara

Makara are sea-creatures from Hindu mythology. They're half land animal, half sea beast- something like an animal mermaid. Some believe it's a myth related to actual extinct animals from ancient times, others believe it's a spirit animal that defends shrines.

The Makara is said to be tenacious and protective of its territory; it is said to guard waterways, entrances not only to shrines but also royal property. It lives in the rivers and in the deltas of the Ganges.

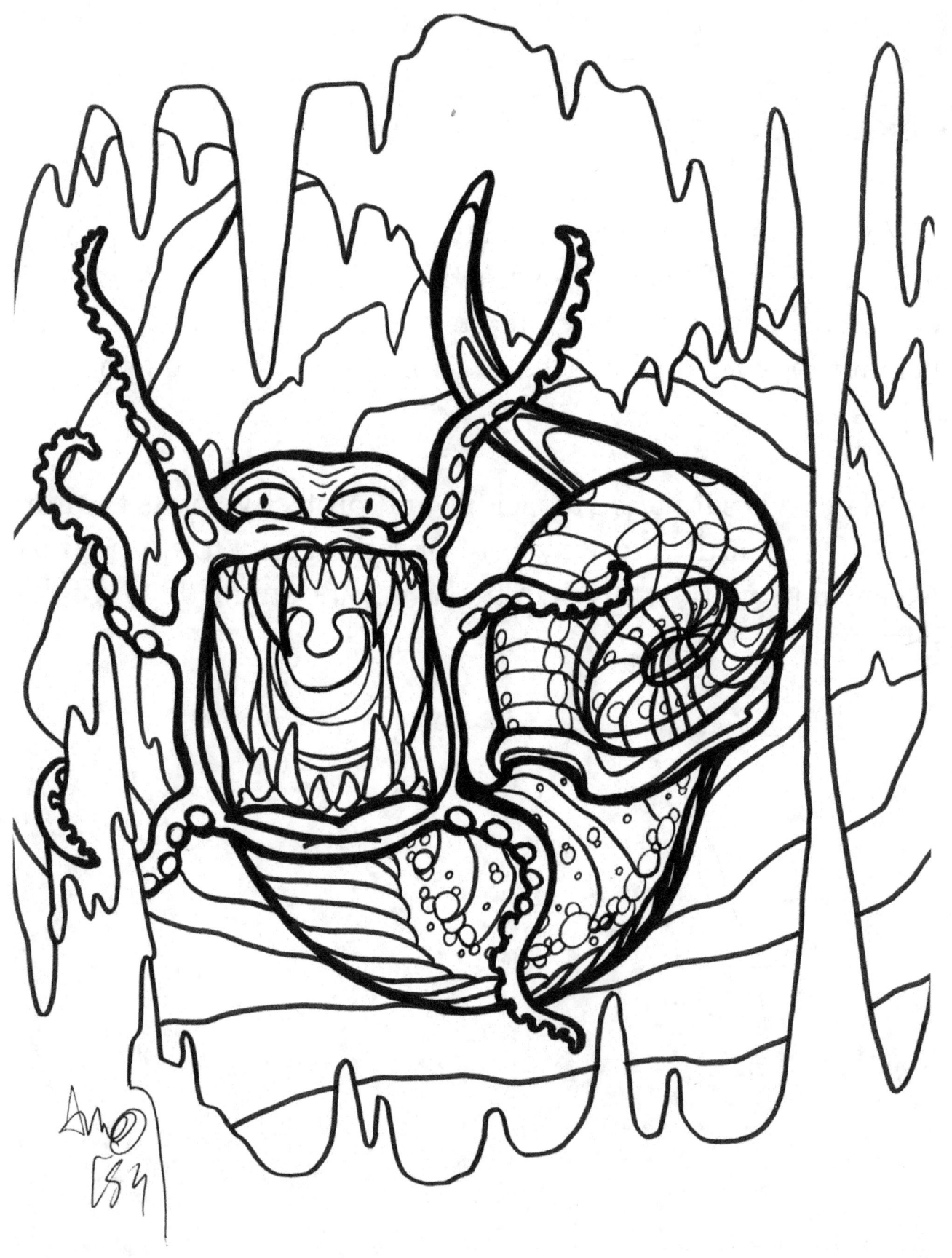

# Lou Carcolh

In French myth, the Lou Carcolh is a serpent that carries a shell on its back like a massive snail. It's said to inhabit caves, and has tendrils, or feelers, along its mouth that can extend up to six miles away.

It uses these tendrils to snare and capture prey outside a cave, then drags the food back into its dark home.

The Lou Carcolh has been blamed for many human disappearances, and is said to swallow its prey whole. If snared by one, the only escape would be to live through being swallowed whole, eventually finding escape by cutting out of the beast from the inside.

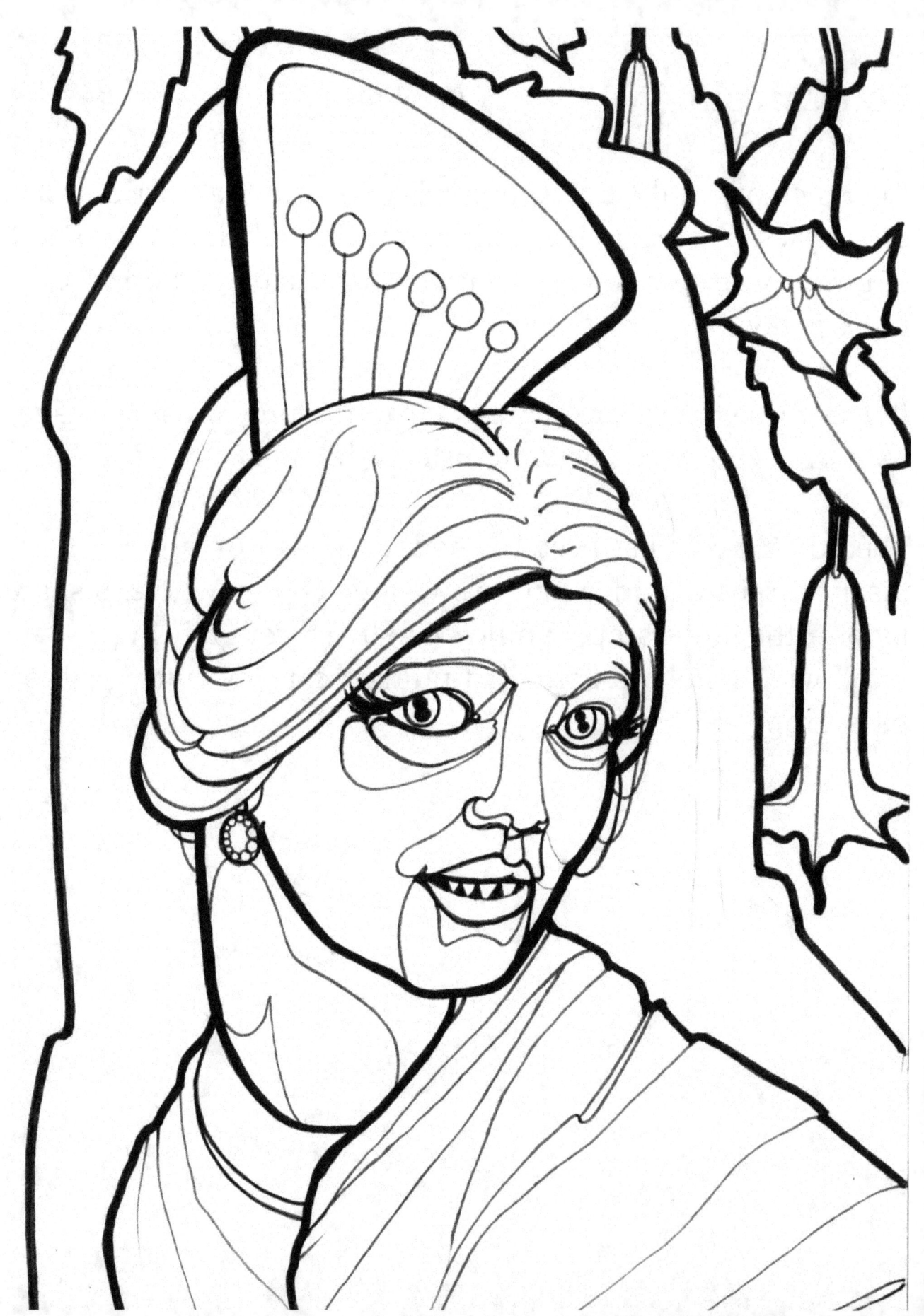

# La Llorona

La Llorona is a legendary ghost from South America. Many presume her to be the ghost of a woman who drowned her own children in order to be with a man, who then rejected her. She drowned herself in grief and cannot pass on fully until she finds her children. So she wanders the earth searching for them.

She has been said to kidnap children who resemble her own lost children, or simply to snatch children who misbehave. She appears at night, weeping and wailing, and walks from lakes or rivers into towns. She drowns the children she steals, so that they will take the place of her own.

La Llorona is described as an older woman, but beautiful. She is tall, has either pure white or pure black hair worn long to her waist, which is sometimes tied in a headpiece. She often is seen wearing a white veil. She has been known to take the form of an aunt or relative, to entice children to follow her to the river or lake.

To be protected from her, Catholics can stay indoors and pray, and she will move on. If outdoors, a flashlight or bright light will dissuade her, as she prefers the dark. Making the sign of the cross with two sticks is also said to drive her away.

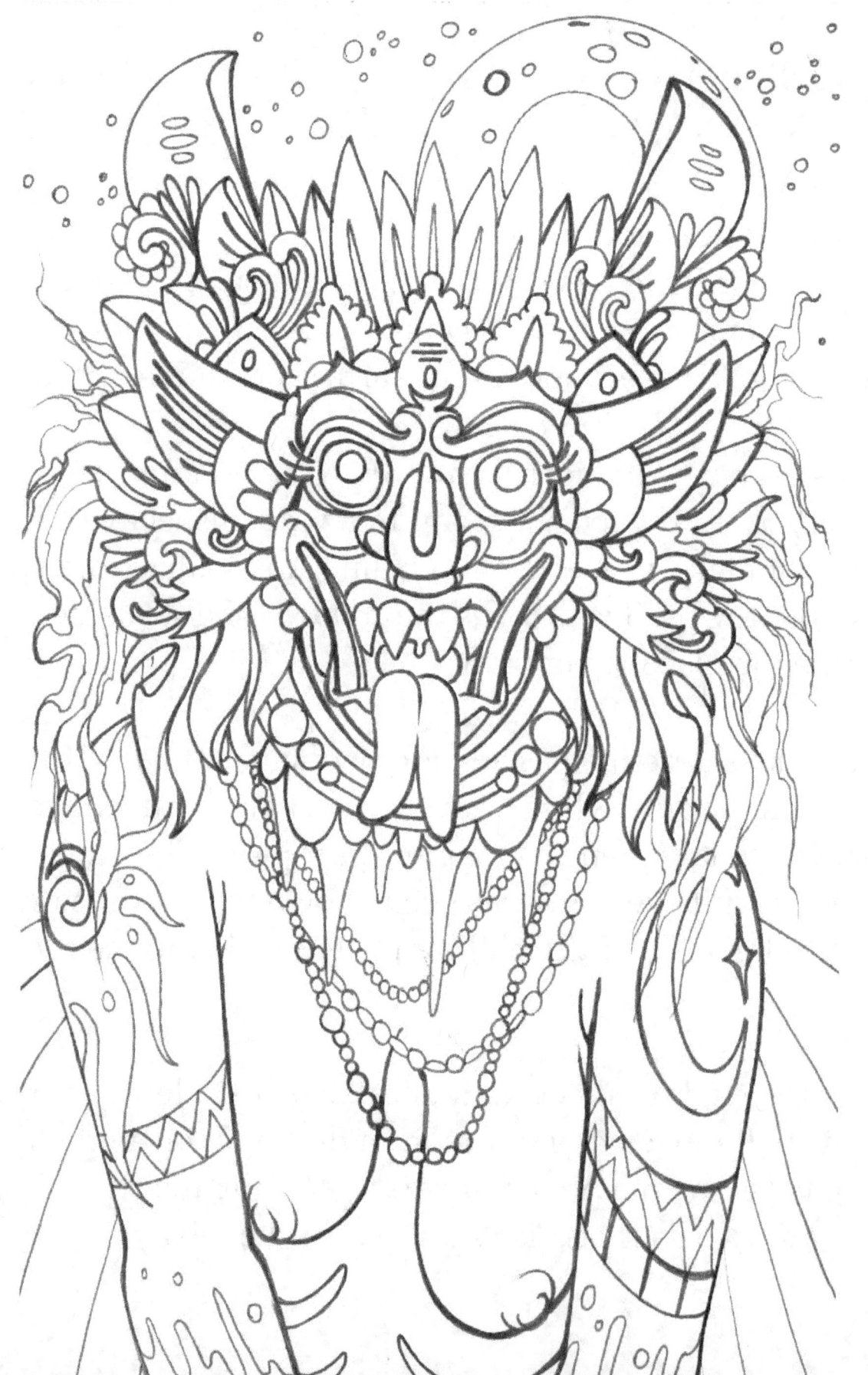

# Rangda

Rangda is a demon queen in Bali. She eats children and steals babies. She's an old woman, with claws and a horrific face. She's a witch, leader of all evil witches.

She has power over plagues, floods, and can destroy crops. Her name means "widow."

There are stories that claim she was a powerful local witch or possibly a mighty queen before becoming supernatural. Balinese villages keep a mask based on her and dance with it in a ceremony to keep her away.

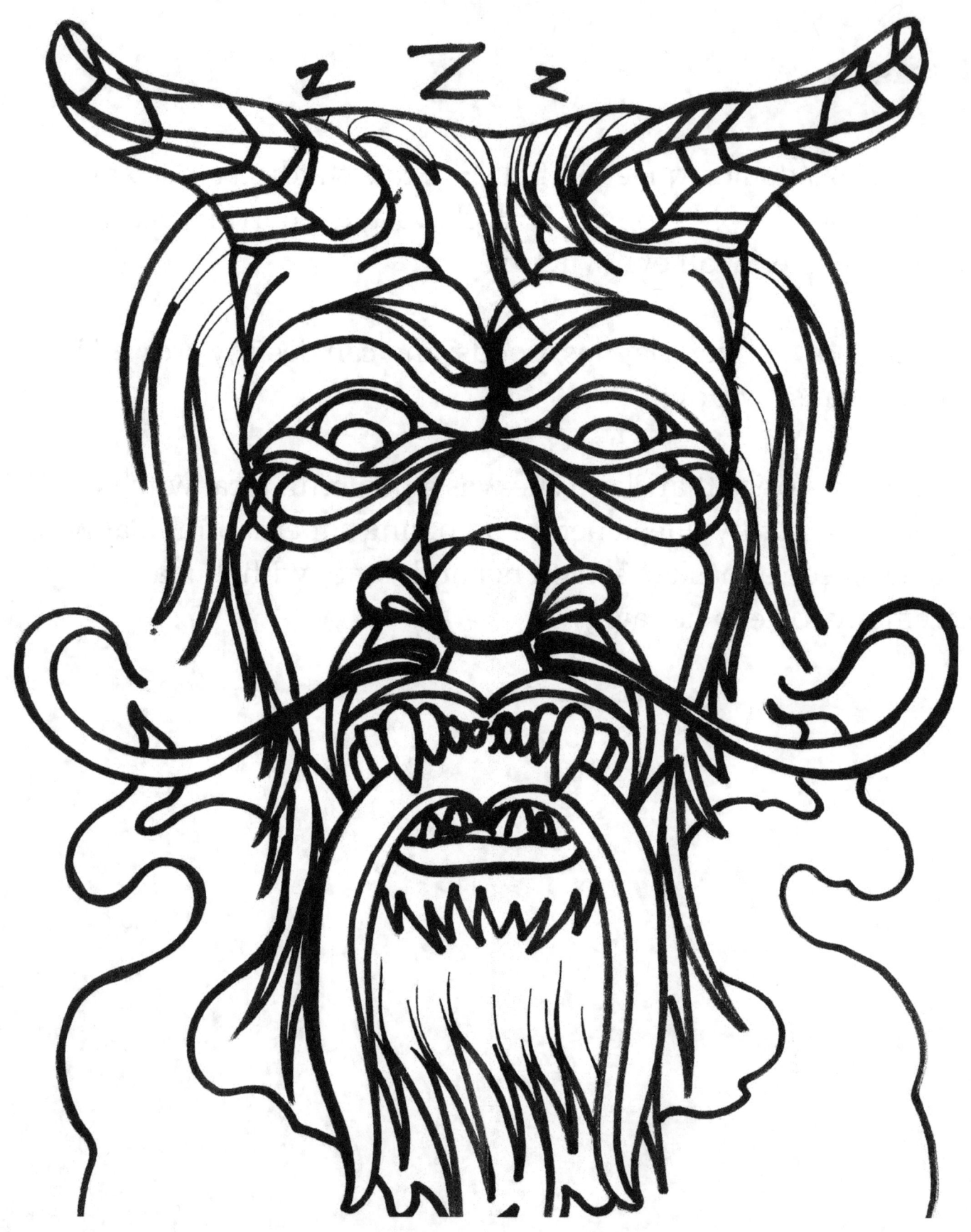

# The Boo Hag

The boo hag is a nocturnal attacker well-known to the Gullah in the southeastern US. It has no skin of its own, and gets it energy by sucking on a sleeping victim's breath. It obtains this breath by riding the victim, causing them to pant with exertion.

The Boo Hag appears when all in the house are asleep and picks a suitable person to ride. They sneak into a house through any crack or small crevice and then crouch over their victim, inducing a nightmare from which the victim can't awaken.

A spot of cool, sky blue paint on the person's body can keep the boo hag away, as can using this paint in rooms or bedposts.

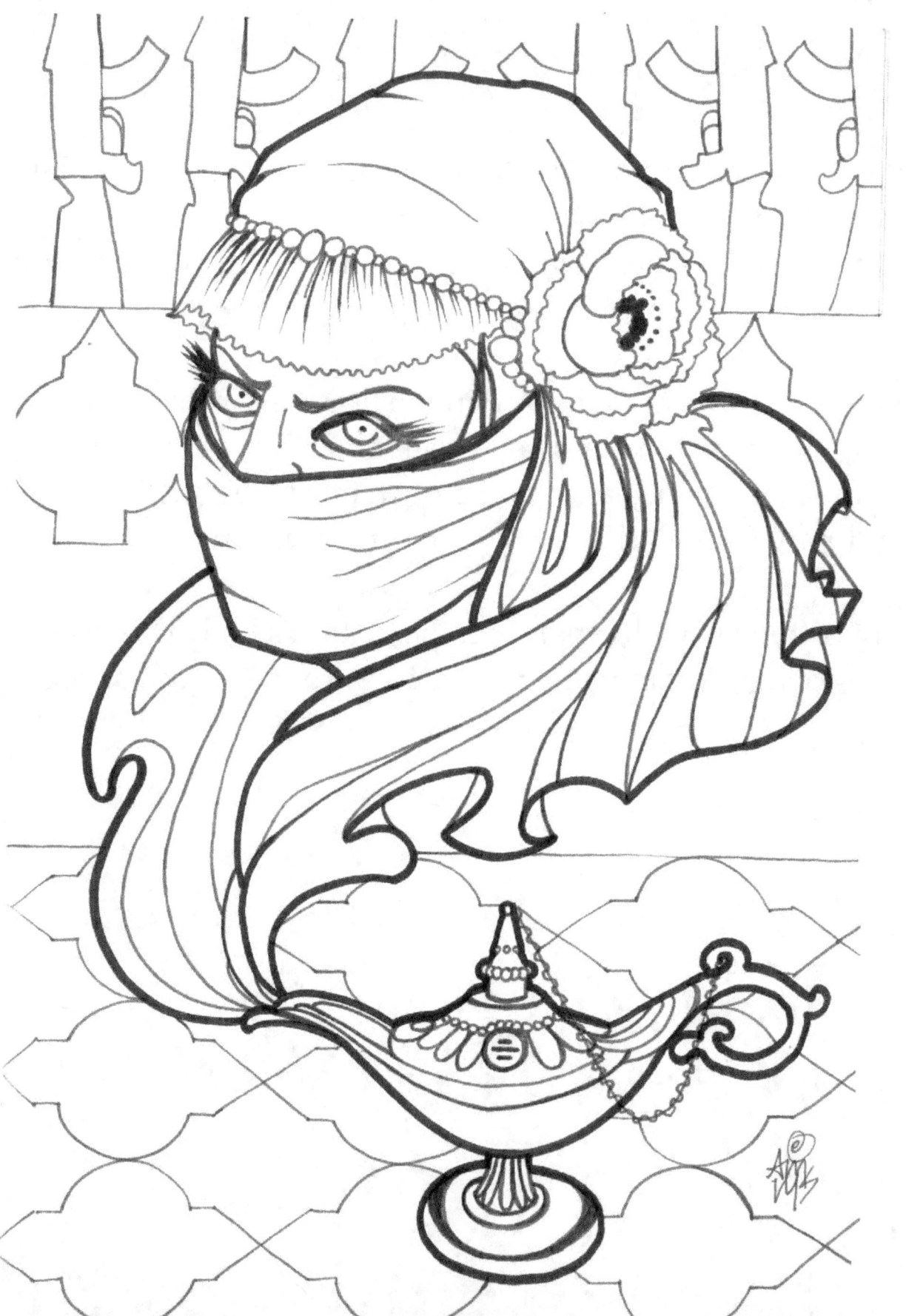

# The Djinn

In Islamic myth, Djinn are supernatural beings made of flames. They appear to humans in any form they choose. They can possess people or they can grant wishes. Djinn are like humans in that they have free will and can be either evil or good in their intent.

In popular culture, djinn are usually seen granting wishes. The fact that they are made of flames is probably why they're usually pictured as being contained in a lamp.

The Djinn may not always grant wishes the way you'd like. There's a tendency in popular folklore to assign mischievous motives to the Djinn; assuming that all wishes will be granted "to the letter" which sometimes have disastrous consequences.

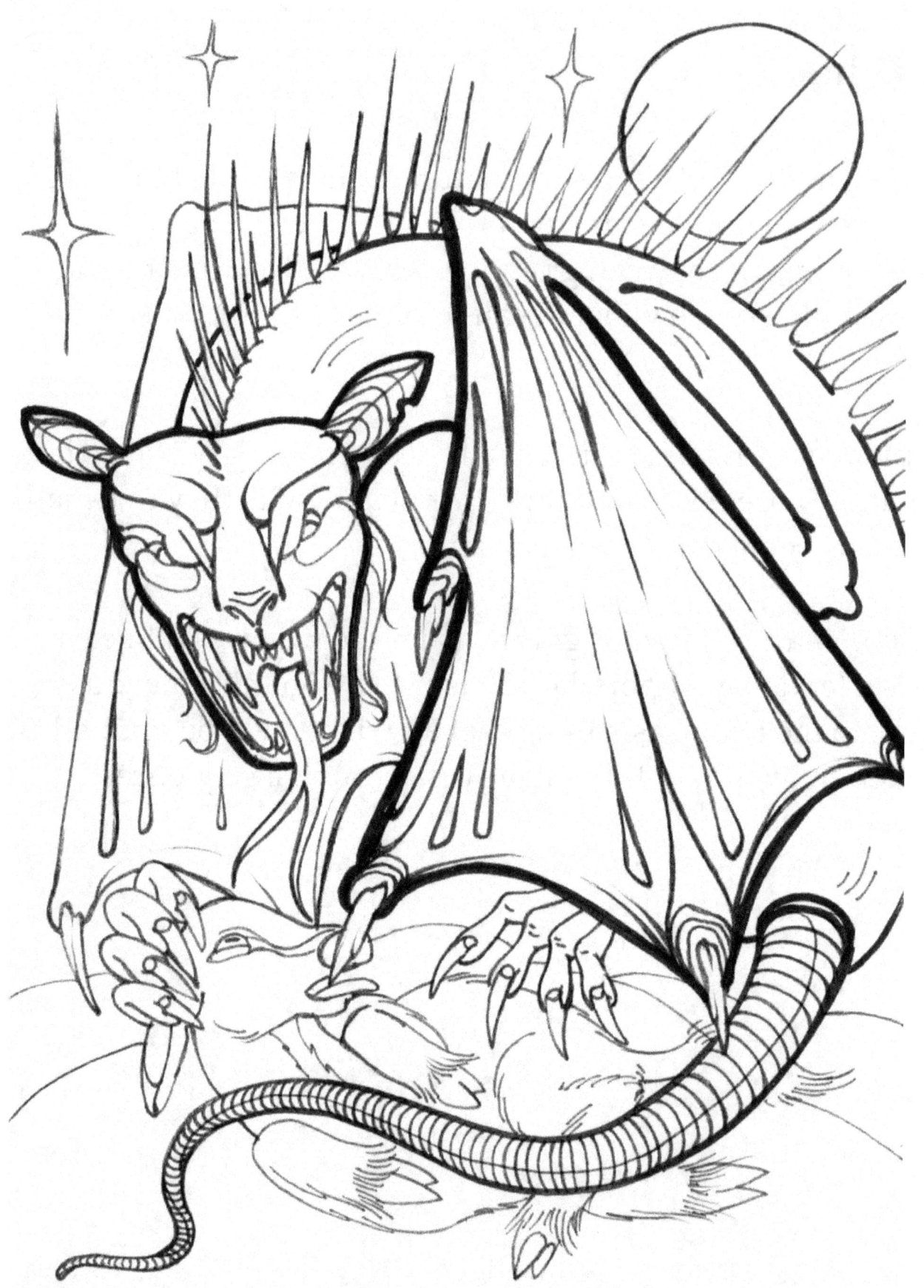

# Chupacabra

Chupacabras are said to be three or four feet tall, with sharp teeth and blazing eyes. They are vicious and usually attack farm animals which are unattended, drinking their blood and tearing them to shreds. They've been reported in South America, Mexico, Puerto Rico, and now Central America and Texas.

Chupacabras prefer to strike goats and sheep, draining them of blood. They're known also as "goat suckers" for this very reason. Some witnesses report that they have wings, others that they are four-legged, moving like coyotes. Said to be able to leap great distances, they'll hiss or screech when startled or injured. They always smell strongly of sulfur. People who have seen the creature explain that it will stand on its hind legs, showing a spiky back and impressive claws. Most run away from it, rather than investigating further.

Chupacabras will often attack animals at night, waking the sleeping farmers from slumber. The Chupacabra is a cryptid, with no supernatural defense systems. Simply shooting it will either kill it or dissuade it from eating the remainder of your goats. Since they are elusive, nocturnal creatures, sightings are not common and killing one is even rarer.

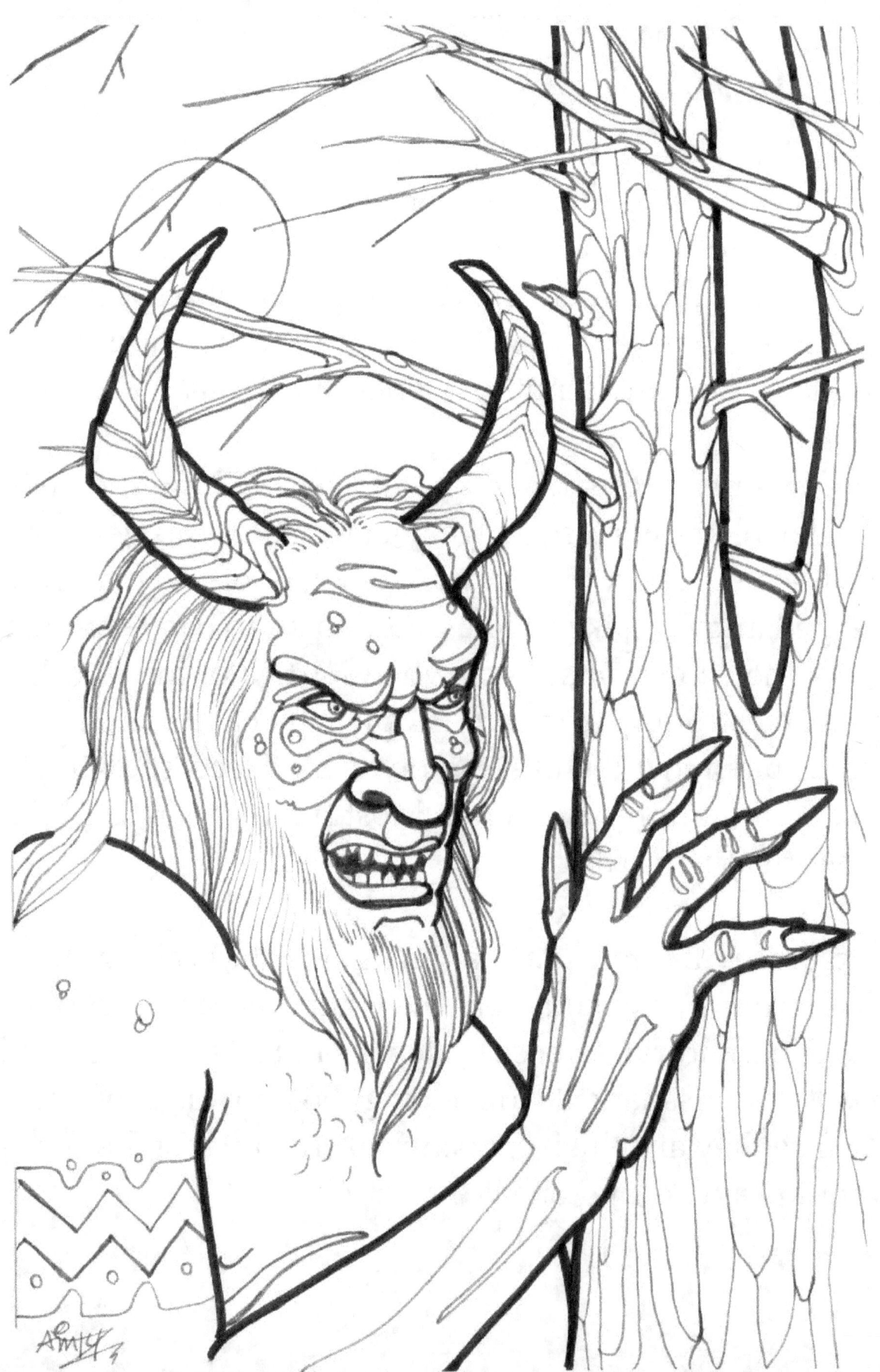

# Trolls

In Scandinavian folklore, Trolls live as far from human beings as they can get. Unlike other supernatural beings, they don't steal people or attack them without provocation, but are extremely territorial.

When human lands expand, Trolls can get angered and cause lots of destruction. Hiking or exploring in unpopulated areas can also arouse their anger. Trolls are also angered by church bells, Christian ceremonies on their land, and roads.

Trolls get angry <u>a lot</u>. This doesn't sound too bad until you realize that Trolls, when angry, throw boulders and sometimes move mountains in anger. They're supernatural earthquakes, therefore people prefer to avoid them altogether.

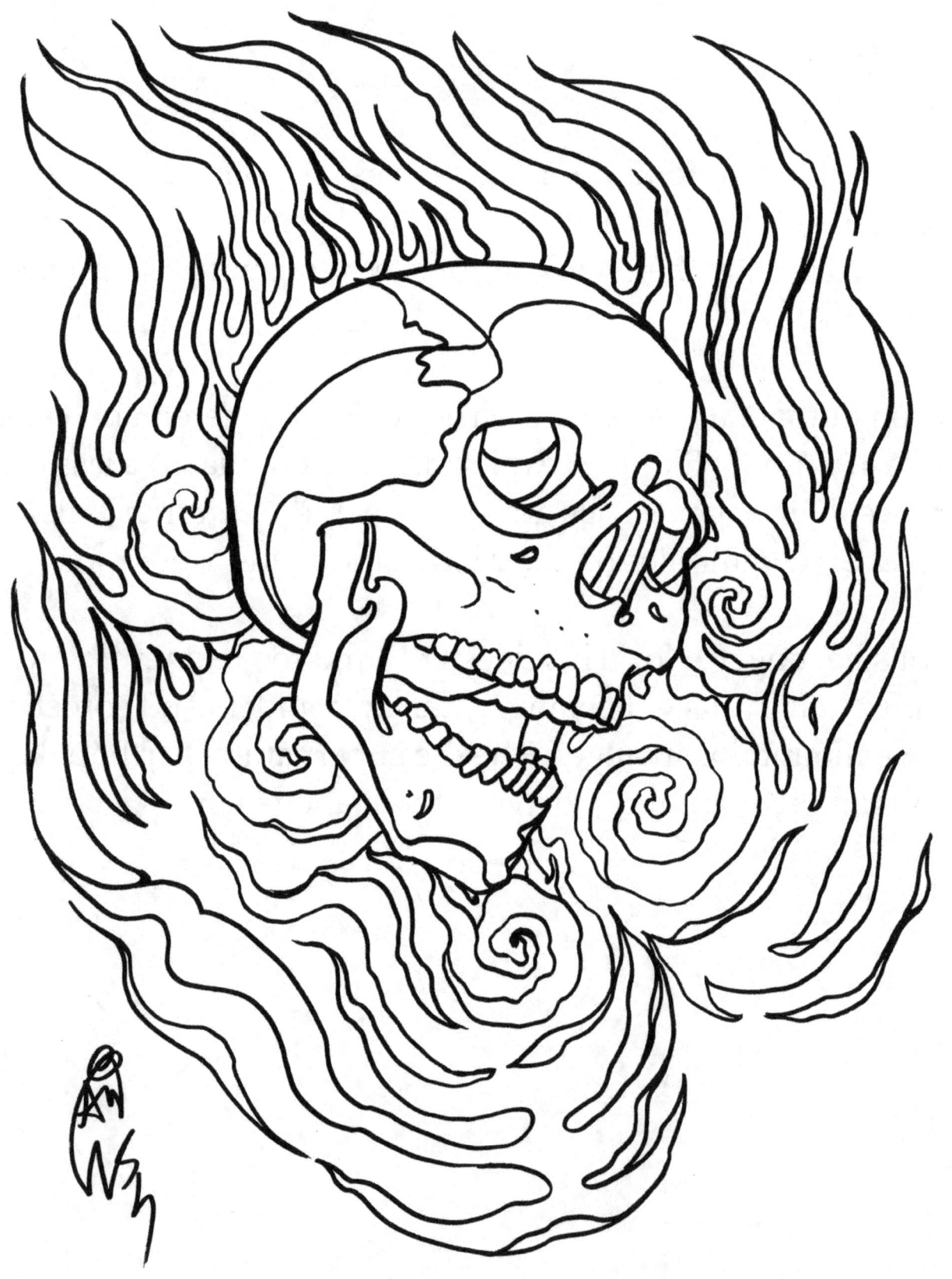

# Kemamang

The Kemamang appears in dark forests in Indonesia. When seen from a distance, it attempts to lure travelers off the path, so that they get lost in the forest. When it's near, it uses fiery balls of light surrounding a skull to frighten passing people.

It feeds on fear and anger, which is easy to find by waiting near well-traveled dark paths and frightening people passing by. In some villages, farmers and workers caught out after dark will stay and work all night, only returning home at dawn, rather than risk an encounter with a Kemamang.

It may spout fire if angered and has been blamed for many forest fires and temples being destroyed. To keep away the Kemamang, don't travel alone after dark on dark paths, or instead go to the nearest mosque and pray before traveling.

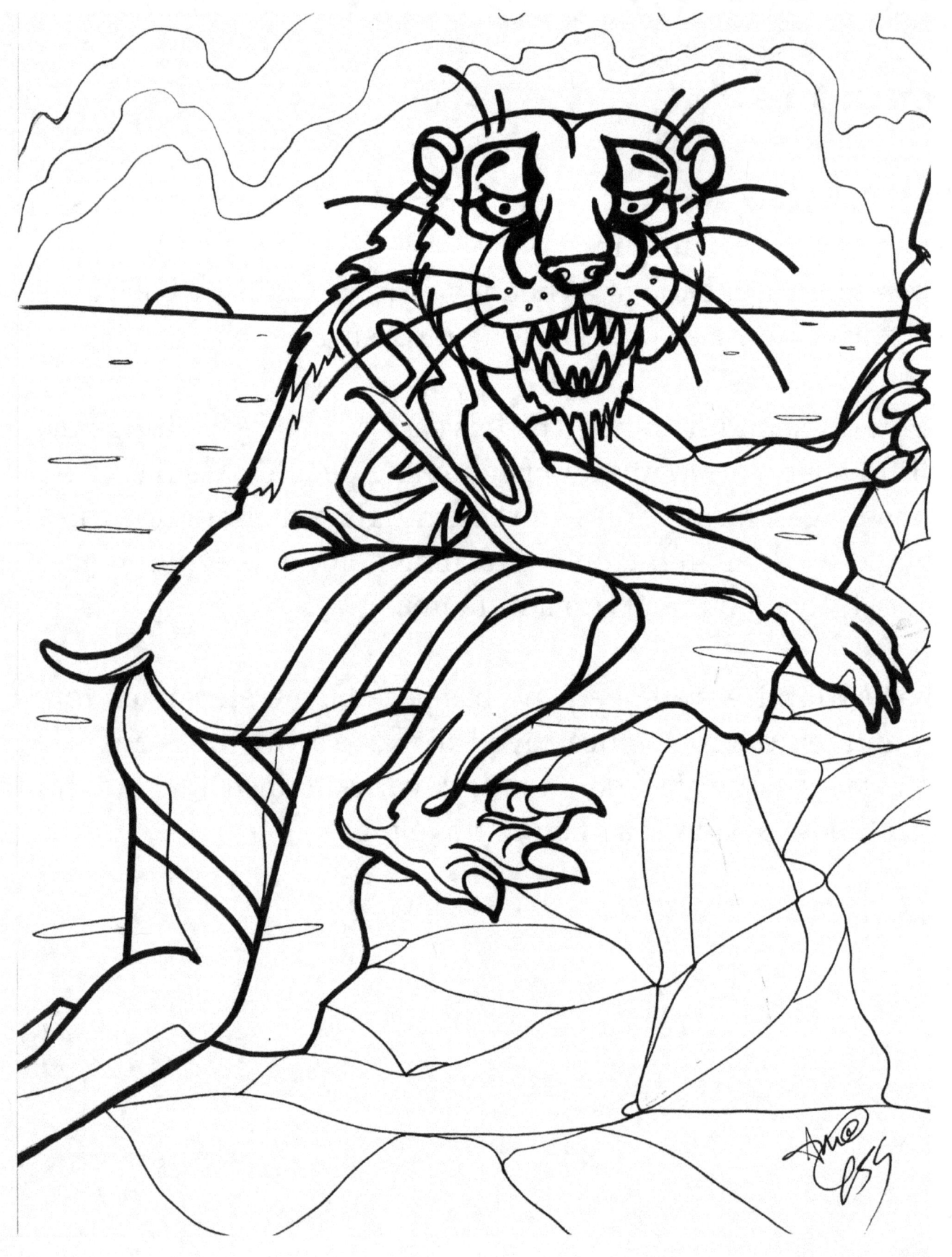

# Kushtaka

The Kushtaka is a Tlingit legend, half-man, and half-sea otter. It is usually male, and appears in or near a lake or pond. When left to its own devices, it feeds on fish and mollusks, just like an otter. When disturbed by humans in its territory, it may become violent. It is known to stack and carry off young women, to eat children, and to simply drown men who pursue it.

In some areas a Kushtaka is regarded as a shape-shifter, who can appear human and mingle with people in order to choose its victims. Just remember that its teeth will always give it away; they do not resemble human teeth, and are pointed and sharp like an otter's teeth.

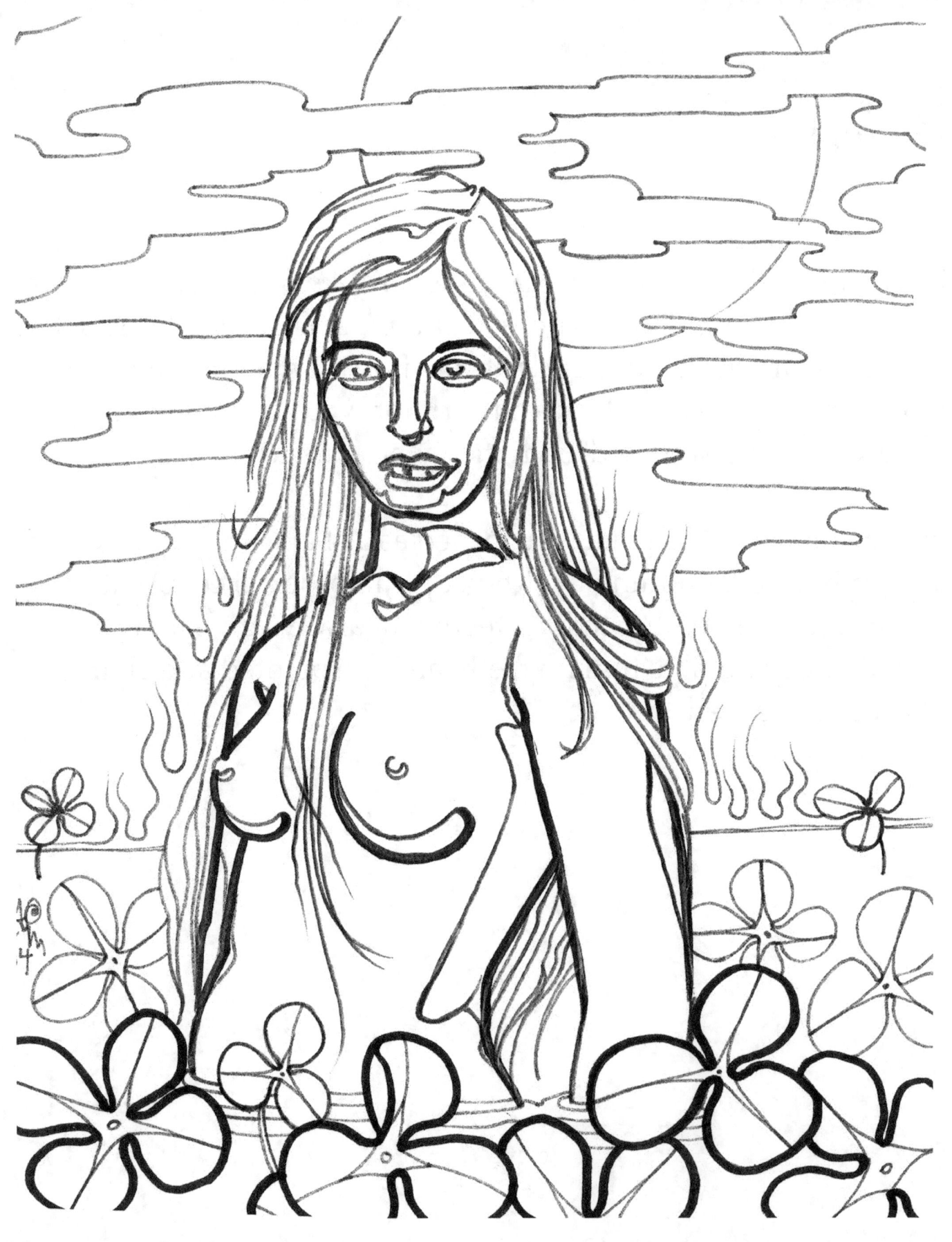

# Jinny Greenteeth

Jinny Greenteeth is a dark sidhe, a wicked fairy. Some believe she is the ghost of a woman murdered in the bog. She's attractive at first, luring you in. Then she will grab you, hold you tight, pull you under, and devour you.

She may pretend to be a drowning woman, in order to get you into the water, or a beautiful nude woman, swimming, enticing you. She haunts rivers, ponds, and bogs.

Some say she is a terrestrial mermaid, cut off from the ocean and forced to stay in freshwater.

The only way to escape her is to look away and not allow her to touch you. Once she's touched you, like weeds, she will wrap around you and bring you under the surface.

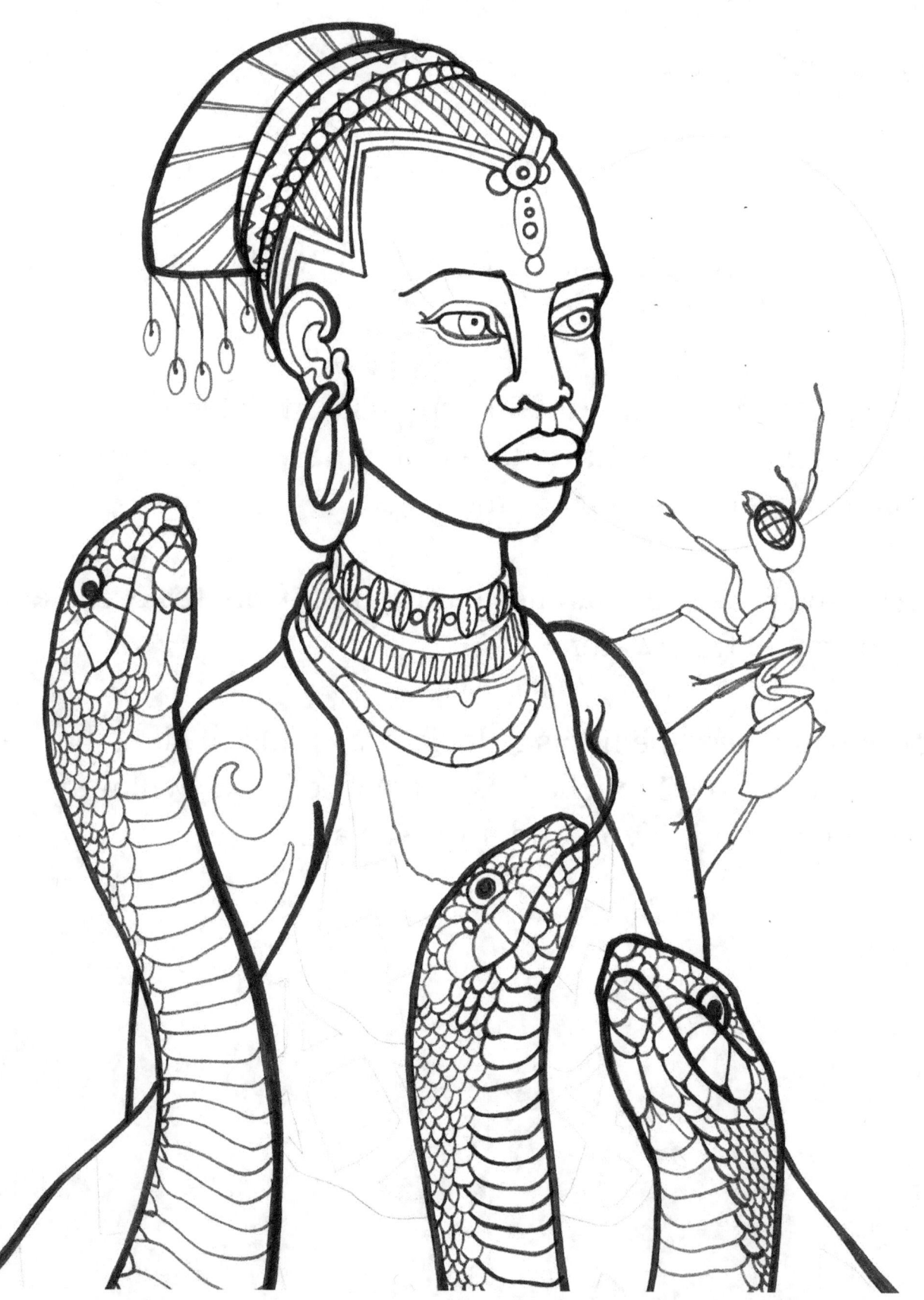

# Ilomba

The name "Ilomba" is from Zambia, but this creature is known throughout Africa. Using blood from an enemy, a witch creates a snake being. To most people, this being looks like a normal snake, usually a harmless one. To the target of the witch's ire, this snake is the Ilomba, a large snake with a human head, the head of its creator.

The Ilomba bites the chosen victim and devours the soul, which gives it strength. The Ilomba must eat regularly, so the witch must point it to more and more victims, target someone new each time it hungers. The lives of the witch and his creation become intertwined; if the Ilomba is killed the witch will die.

When the witch has run out of victims, the Ilomba will turn on its creator and devour it. It can only be killed by someone who is not its intended target, so once an Ilomba has been set on you, there's no escape except for killing the witch or wizard who created it.

The fact that snakes are so common in Zambia makes this tale all the more frightening. At any time you could be right next to one of these creatures and not even know it. Like many other monsters in mythology, the Ilomba hides in plain sight.

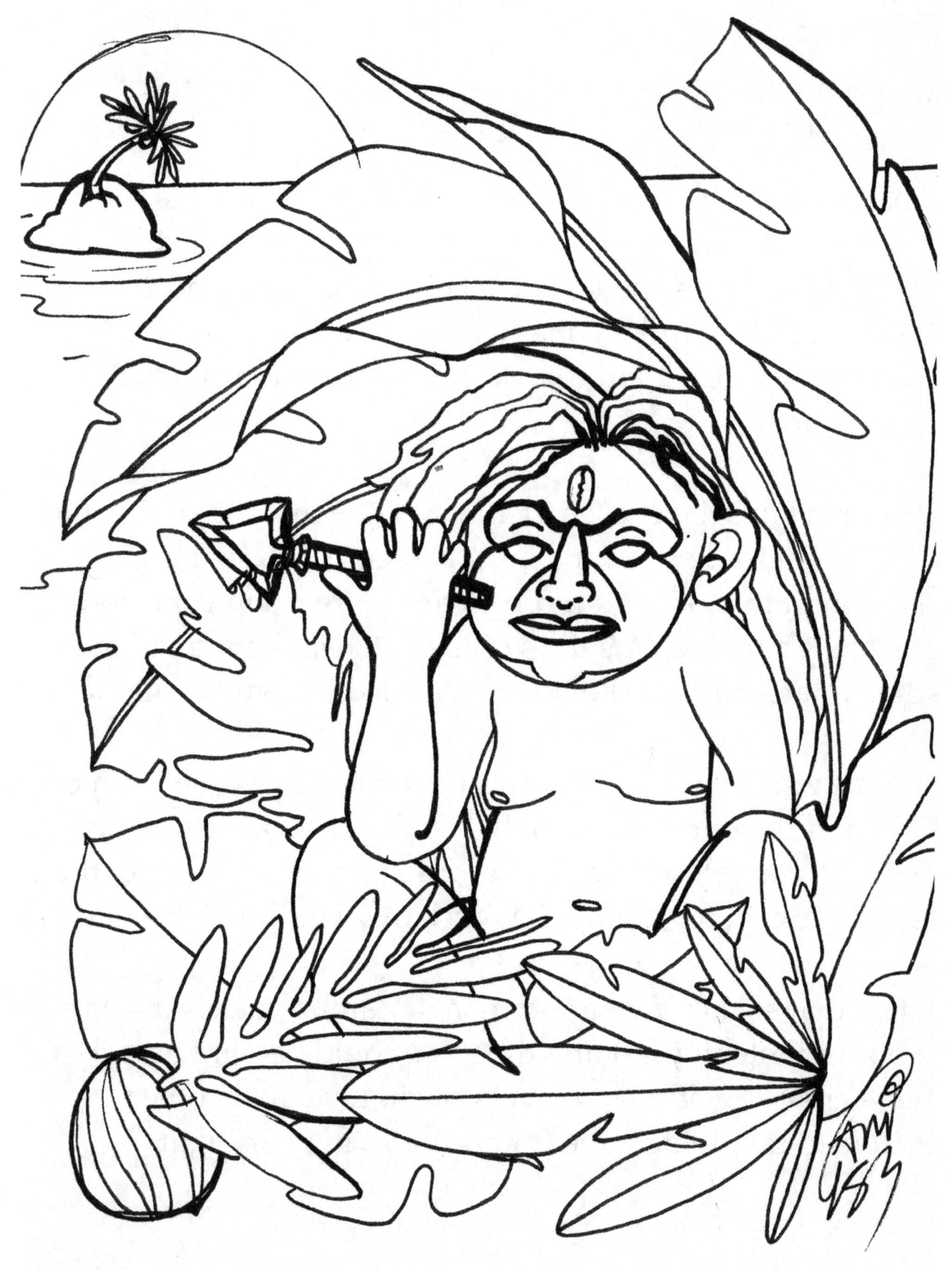

# Menehune

The Menehune are cryptids. They're an ancient race of people said to once have lived in Hawaii and other Pacific Islands. They're said to still inhabit deep forests and untouched areas of the islands.

They are tiny in stature, less than three feet tall, and evidence of them can be seen in many tiny huts and buildings hidden in the forests. They're said to have built fish traps, ponds, roads, boats, and all kinds of houses.

It's believed they lived on the islands before the native peoples. Their small structures can be found all over the islands to this day. It's said that disturbing their current territories can cause them to get violent, throwing pebbles or shooting small poisoned arrows at intruders.

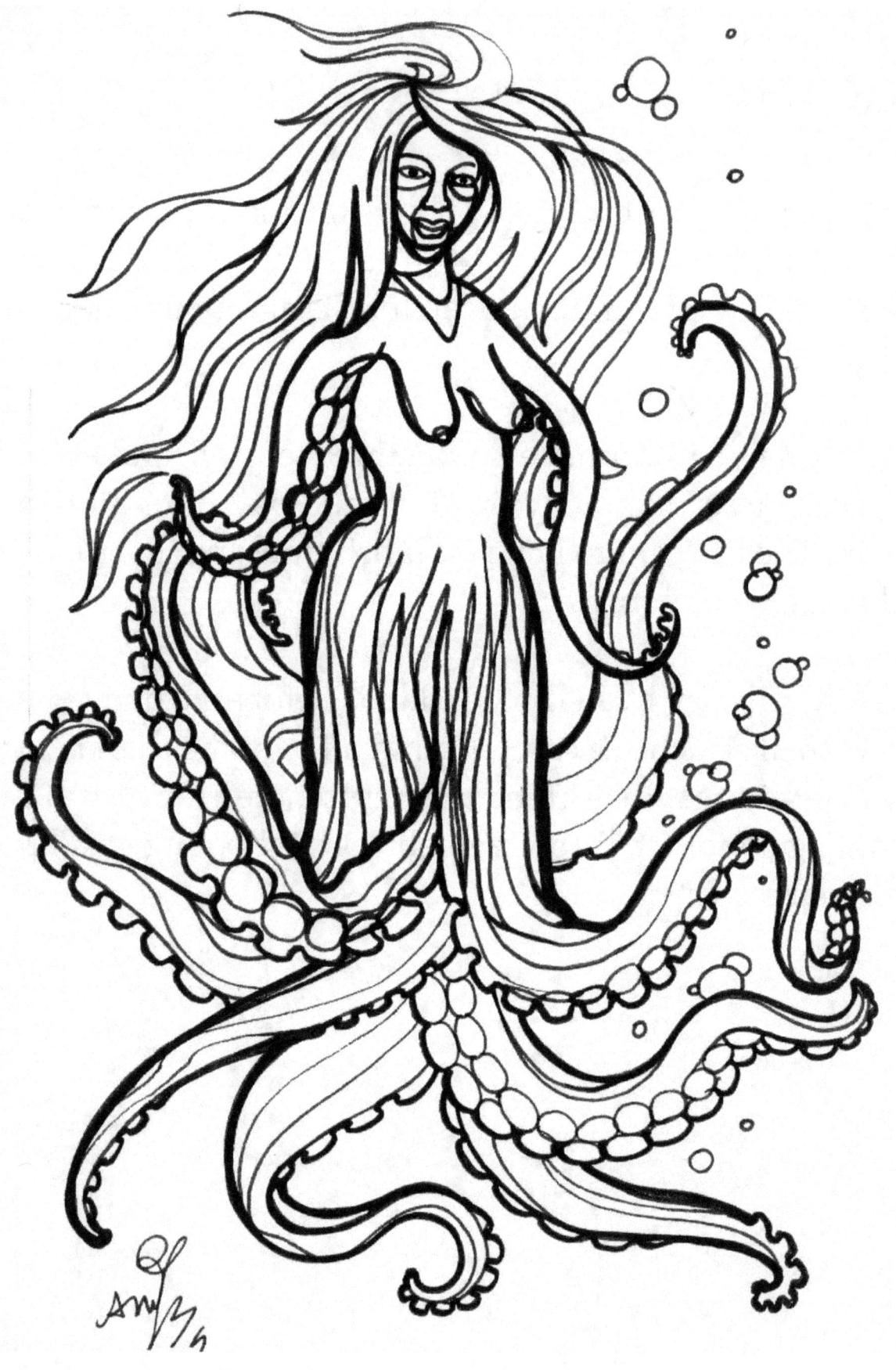

# Migas

The Migas, from Central Africa, is known as a river creature that brutally attacks those on riverbanks. It prefers to attack children by hiding in rocks and brush near the bank before braining them. It also overturns canoes and attacks those inside.

It's an intelligent creature, like a human being; but its body is soft like an octopus, with tentacles in places of its lower body. It uses a beak to feed, and its human-like head is merely exists for appearance.

It can be avoided by staying in open areas along riverbanks, rather than among rocks. It can be killed by spearing or shooting, since it's a cryptid.

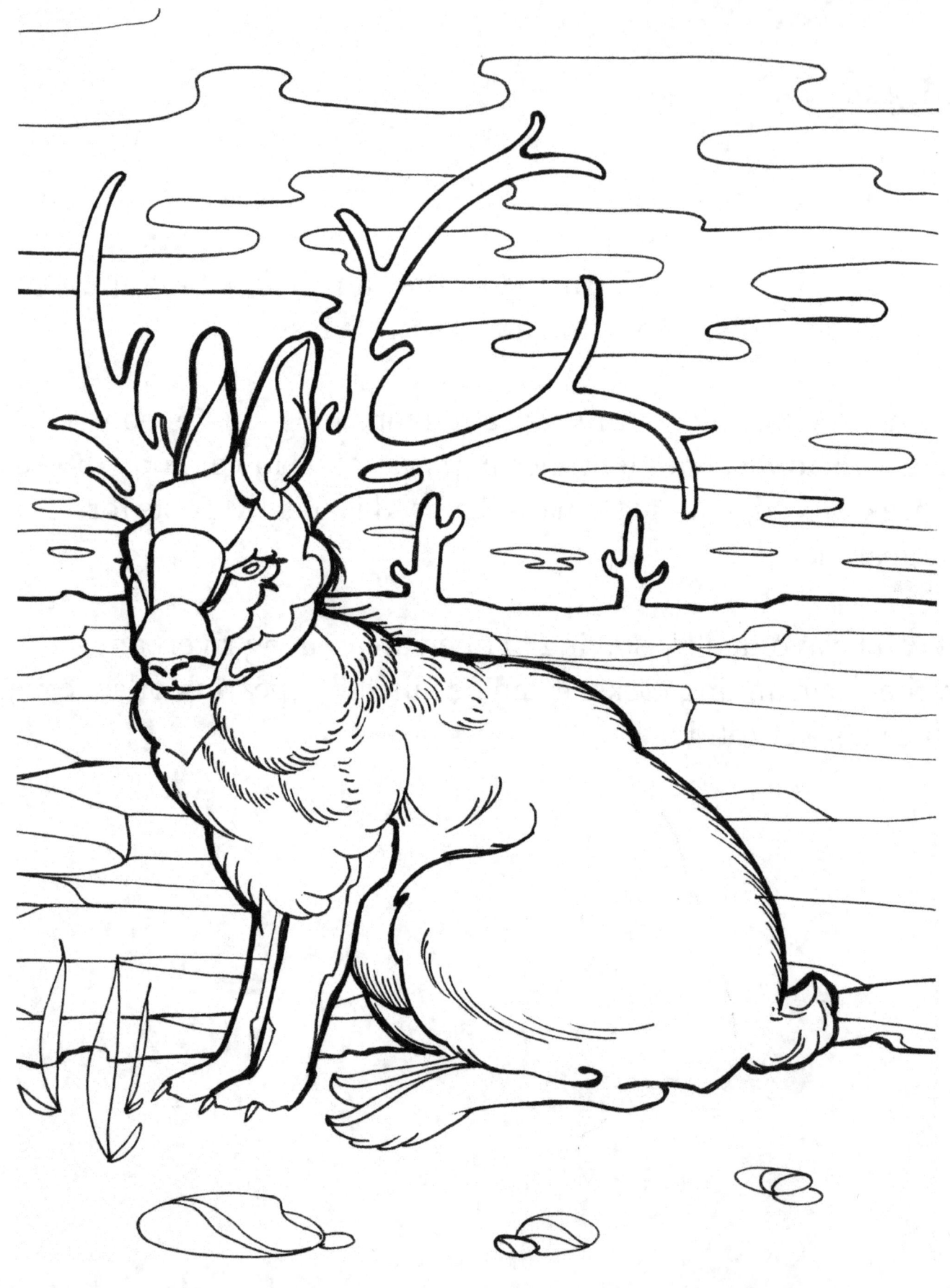

# Jackalope

The Jackalope is an antlered, sometimes winged, jackrabbit. It's found in the southwestern United States.

A Jackalope is fast as an antelope, and as camouflaged as a jackrabbit. You can get hunting tags for them in Wyoming every year; make sure to remember when hunting a Jackalope, it's important to wear good, high leather boots. Jackalopes can be dangerous and may try to gore your legs or savage you with their horns.

The Jackalope can imitate human voices, it has been known to lure hunters away from their fires at night by calling for help. They also find the scent of whiskey irresistible, so traps baited with glasses of whiskey are a good way to capture these elusive beasts.

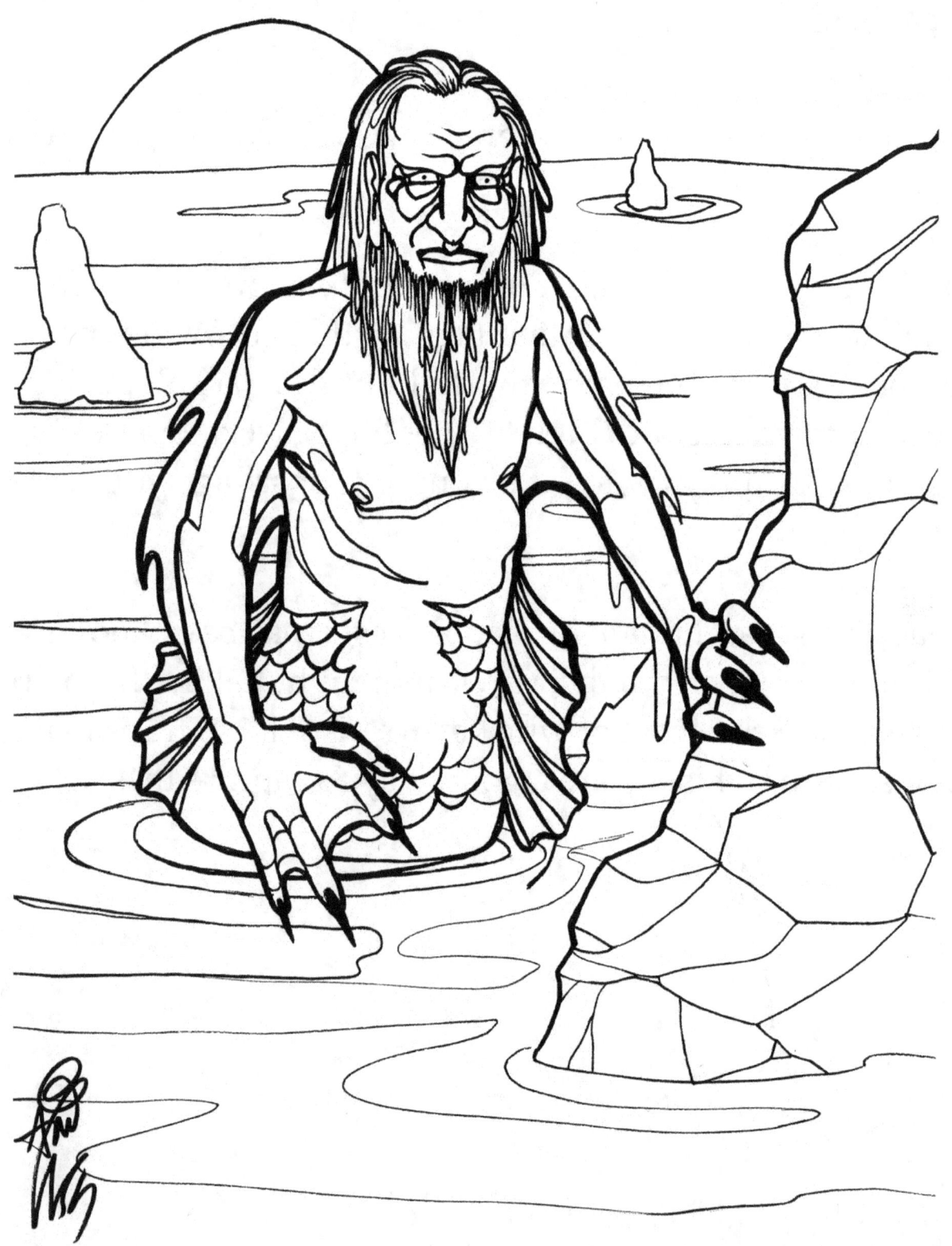

# Vodianoi

These creatures are supernatural beings in Slavic nations. In Russia, they're called Vodianoi. It's common for them to be extremely aggressive and malevolent, attacking any swimmers they notice.

Vodianoi live in deep pools in lakes or rivers, and dislike bragging and boasting. Any swimmer showing off in their hearing range is a target; of which they will attack the person and drown him.

Vodianoi can be kept away by several means. You can drown a drunken stranger as an offering to them, or if you're fishing and not swimming, you can offer them the first catch you make each day.

Since Vodianoi rarely attack fishermen, this second method seems to work well.

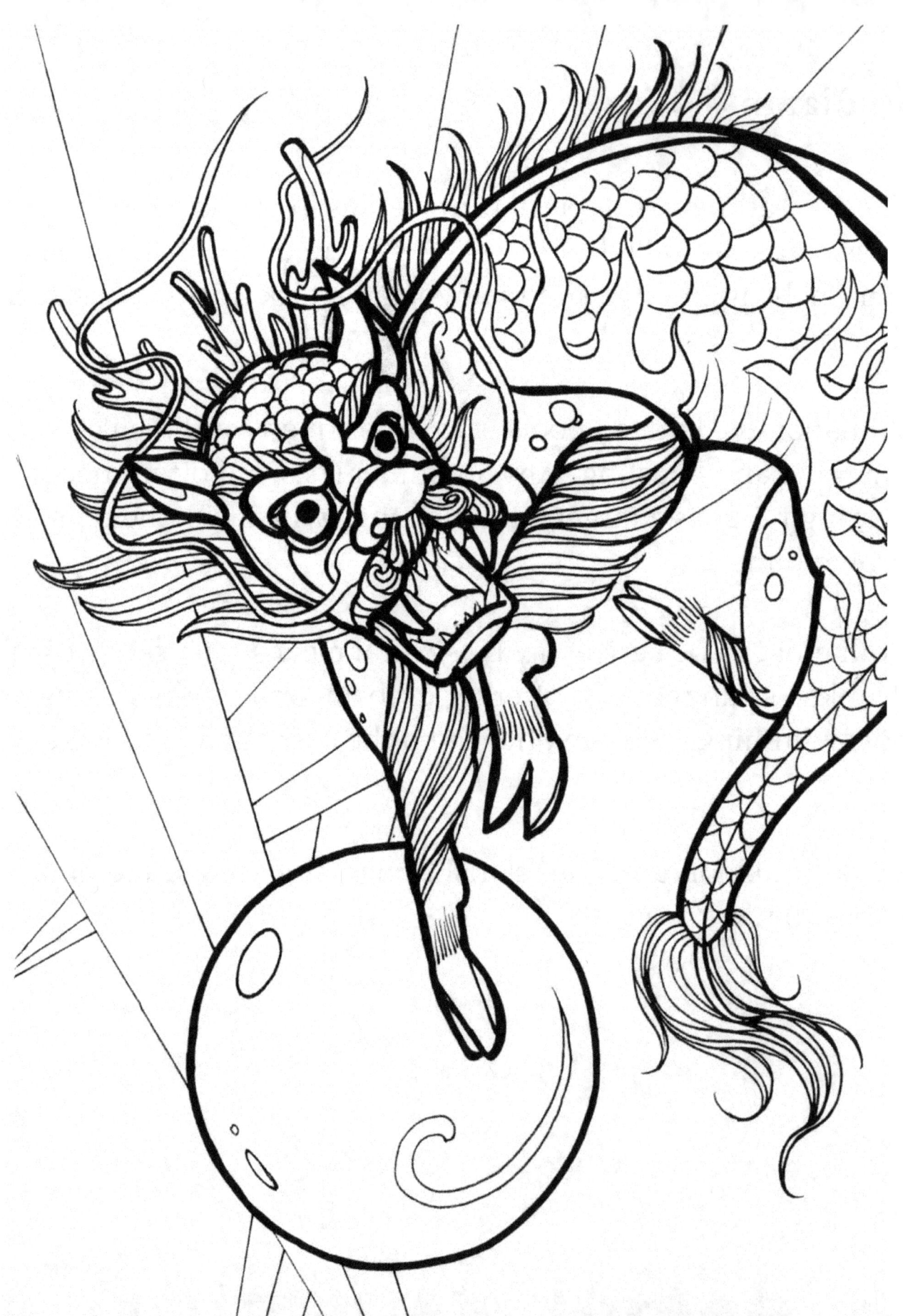

# Kirin

The Kirin is an ancient Chinese myth, a creature which often presages the death of a leader or important person.

A Kirin also punishes the wicked. Its idea of wickedness is not the same as ours, as it follows its own rules. It can breathe heat and flames, and has cloven hooves. It becomes aggressive when a good person is threatened by a bad one.

The Kirin legend is very old and has many variations. It's been regarded as one of the most powerful supernatural beings in some places, along with the dragon and phoenix.

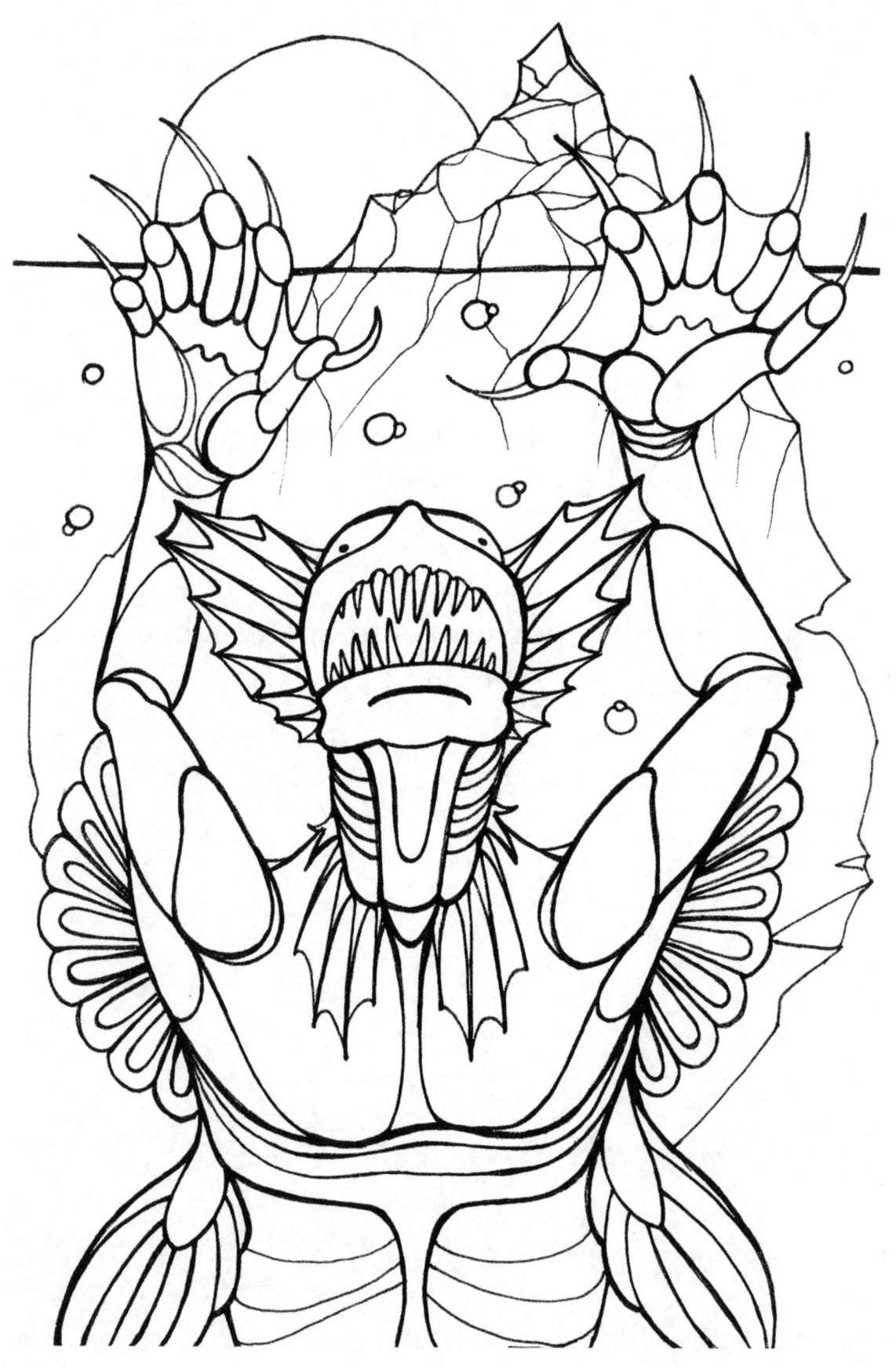

# Ningen

Ningen are the only cryptid in Antarctica. They're pale, white like the ice in the ocean where they live. They have finned hands, and no other facial features than eyes and mouths. Some claim they have legs, others that they have a whale-like tail.

They're usually seen at night, from a boat. There are almost no photographs of them, and very few reports of sightings. However for the area in which they live, there are few people and fewer still looking into the waves.

The first sightings were during the 1990s, as more people were working in the Antarctic. They're massive creatures, between 60 and 90 feet long. Most claim they have hands, like human hands, with five fingers.

No ningen has yet been captured, dead or alive.

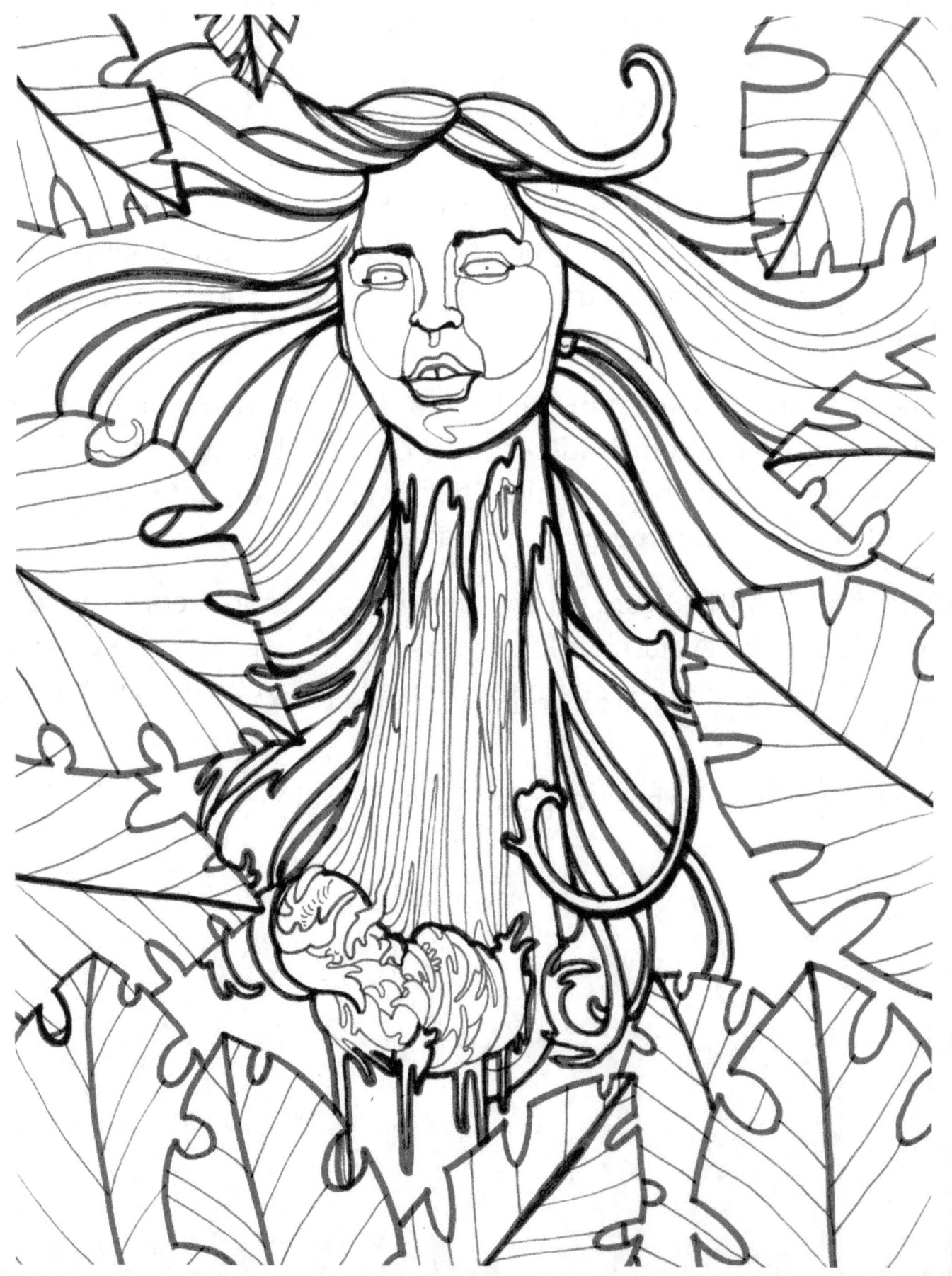

# Krasue

The Krasue is a Thai monster that feeds on entrails, fetuses, placenta, and babies. It's therefore very dangerous to pregnant women, and people put thorny branches around the house to keep it away when someone in the home is pregnant.

It glows red, and floats. The Krasue lives as a normal person during the day, but at night its head and entrails separate from its body, which it leaves hidden away from view. It must go back to its body by daylight and reattach itself.

While of Thai origin similar beings are known throughout Southeast Asia. In all cases, they eat fetuses out of the womb; if it those are available, it eats animals' guts or feces. Any clothing left outdoors overnight to dry may find the mark of a Krasue, as it will wipe its mouth on them, leaving slime, blood, and gore behind.

Some say the Krasue is a witch, who cast the wrong incantations and is cursed. Others believe it's a woman who killed someone in a previous lifetime, who had an abortion, or who is jealous that she
can't get pregnant. Still others believe it to be a ghost or supernatural creature, lacking any humanity.

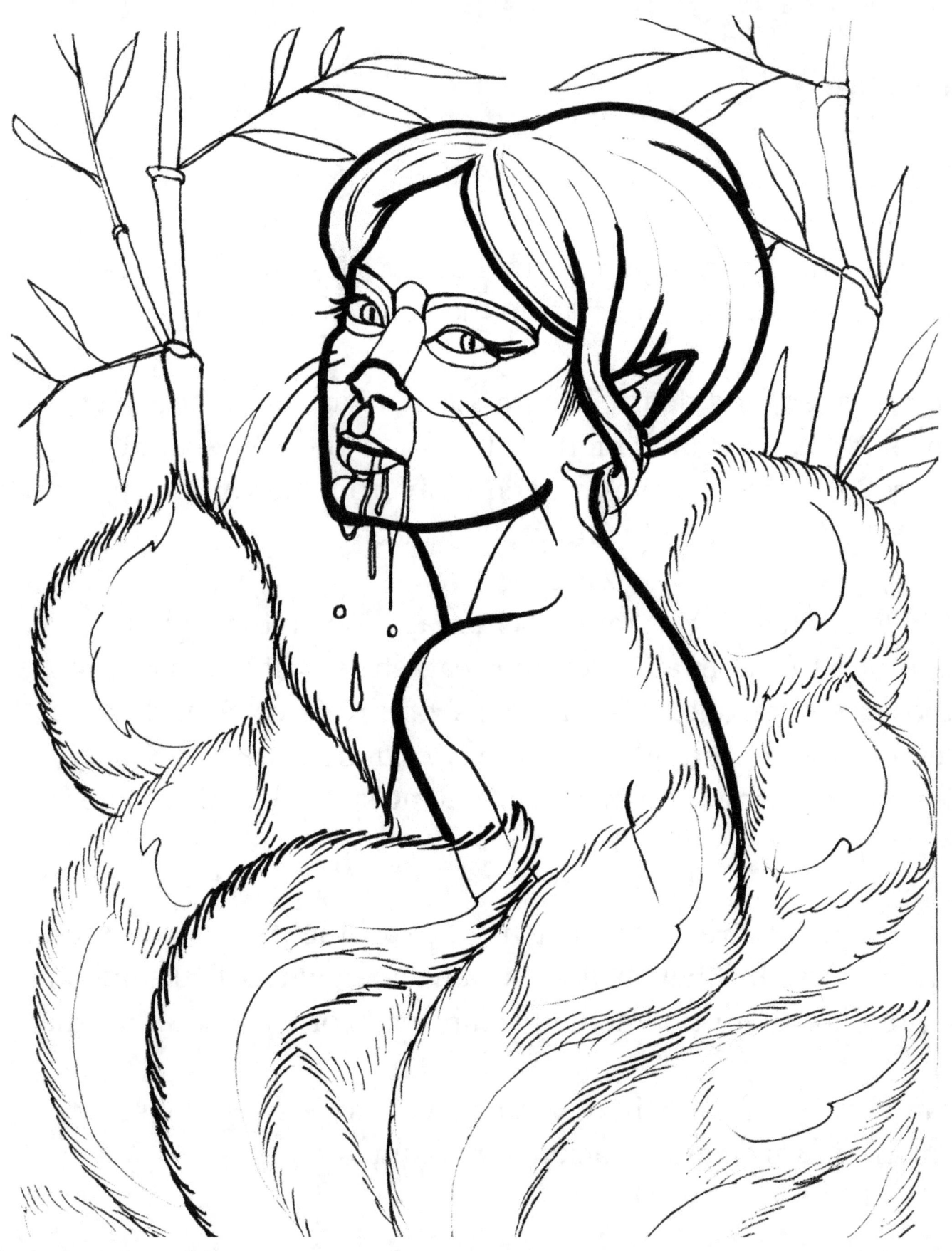

# Nogitsune

In Japanese folklore, a Nogitsune is a woman who is a magical, evil being that's actually a nine-tailed fox. The fox in Japanese folklore is similar to the wolf in European legends; dangerous, tricky and wild. The older the fox is and the more powerful, the more tails it will have.

A common theme is that any woman, encountered alone after dusk, is a fox being. They have trouble hiding their tails and can be caught this way. They also hate and fear dogs; reverting to their fox form and running away if dogs are present.

Nogitsune feed on the life spirit of people, sometimes through sexual contact. They're described as leeches or similar to vampires.

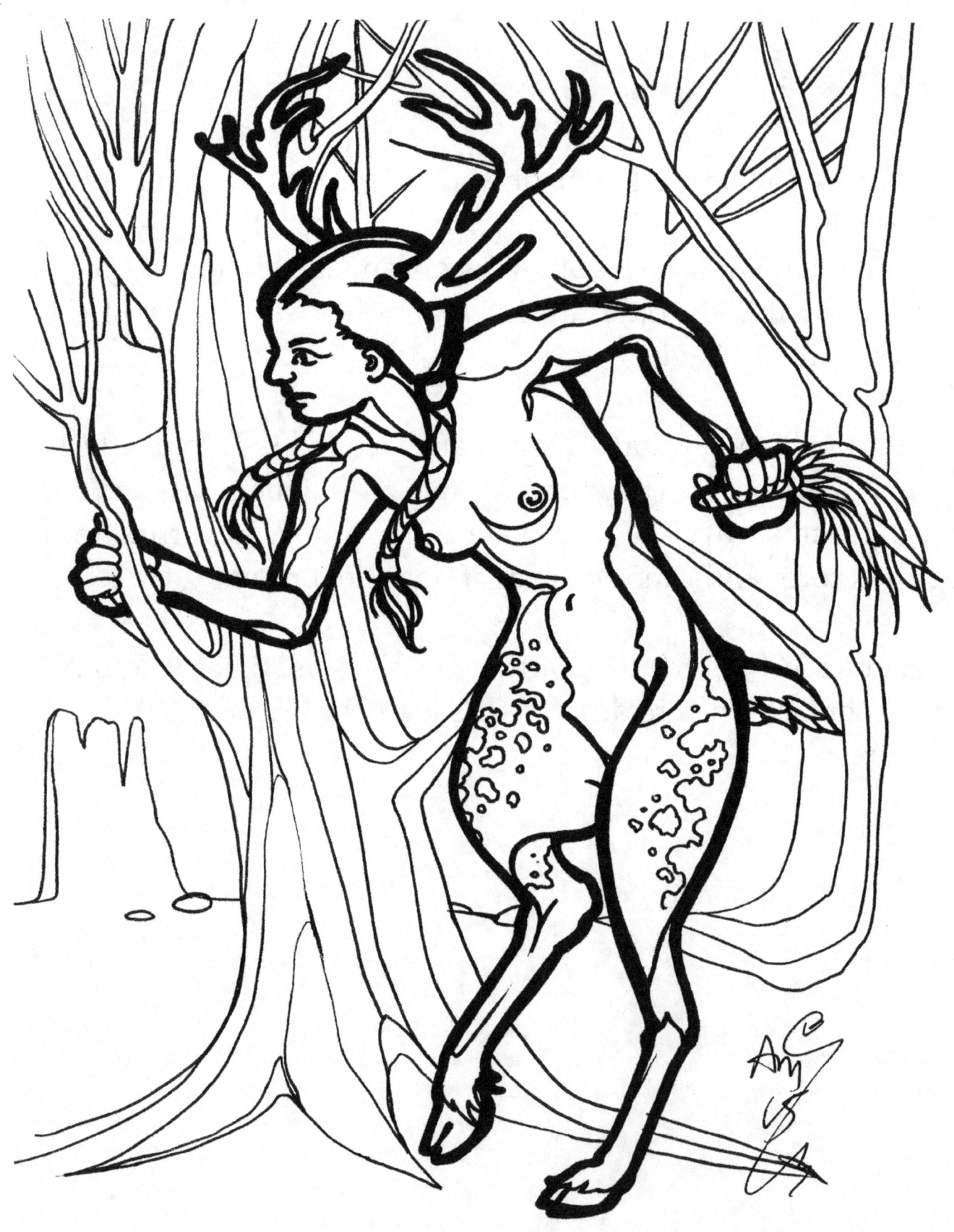

# Deer Woman

Deer Woman is a shape-shifter in Native American folktales in the Pacific Northwest. She's considered beautiful, at least the human part of her.

She lures men from the trail, and then stomps them.

She likes drums and dancing, as well as parties. She will appear at a pow-wow or dance and join in, her lower half covered by a skirt until she's discovered. If any men take liberties with her, she will trample them to death. If she's not discovered at the dance, she will stay until all the drums have ceased.

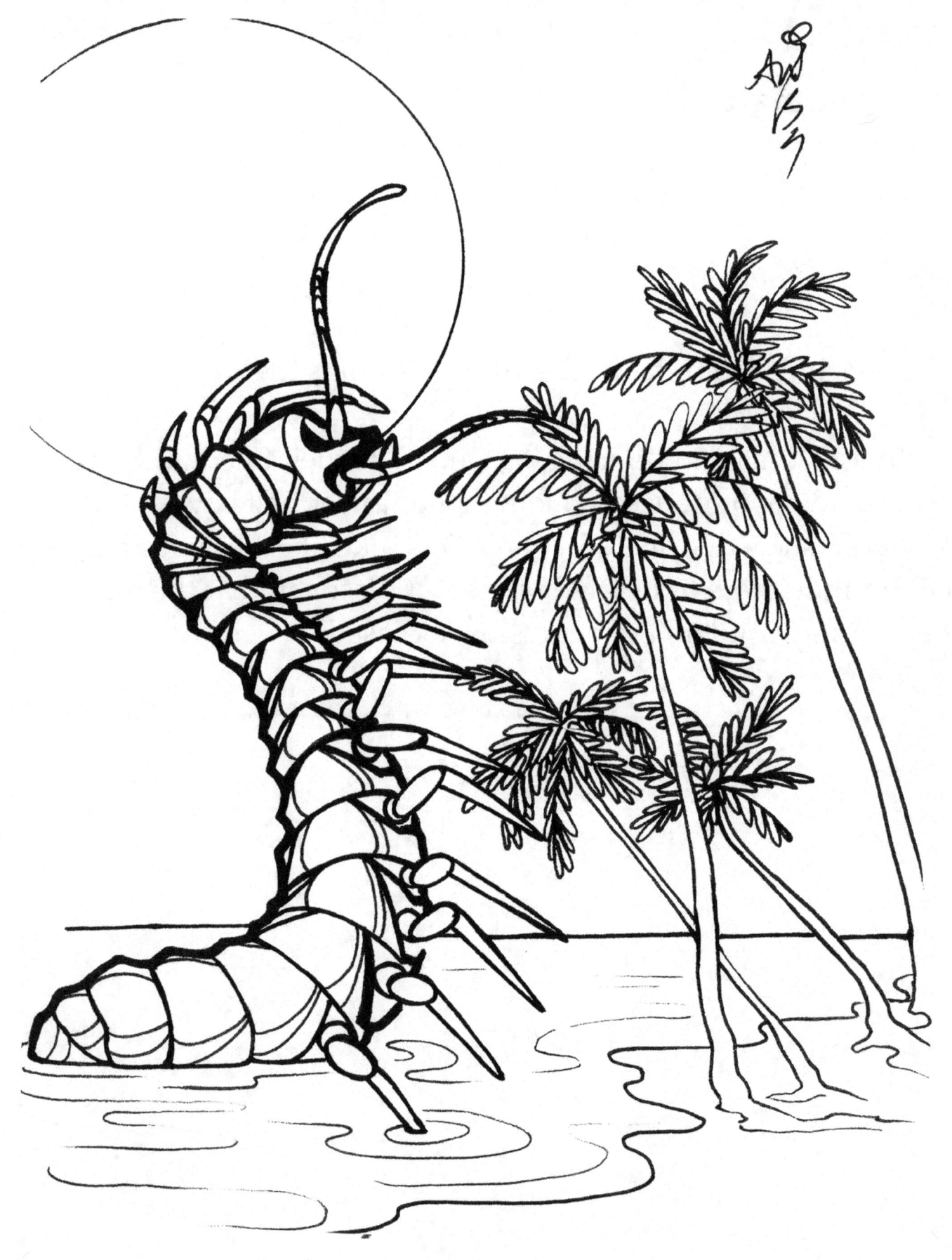

# Con Rit

In Vietnam, a cryptid known as the Con Rit terrorizes boats and divers. It's a gigantic centipede which lives in the coastal waters there and sometimes even upriver.

Remains of a Con Rit washed ashore in the late nineteenth century, but were unfortunately lost. Sightings of this giant creature continue to this day; of which travelers in small boats near the coastline see it most often.

One sighting claimed the animal was 135 feet long, and another claimed that a large centipede swam along, keeping up with the boat. Scientists who research cryptids think it may be a form of giant isopod or other segmented ocean invertebrate, which has successfully eluded capture to this day.

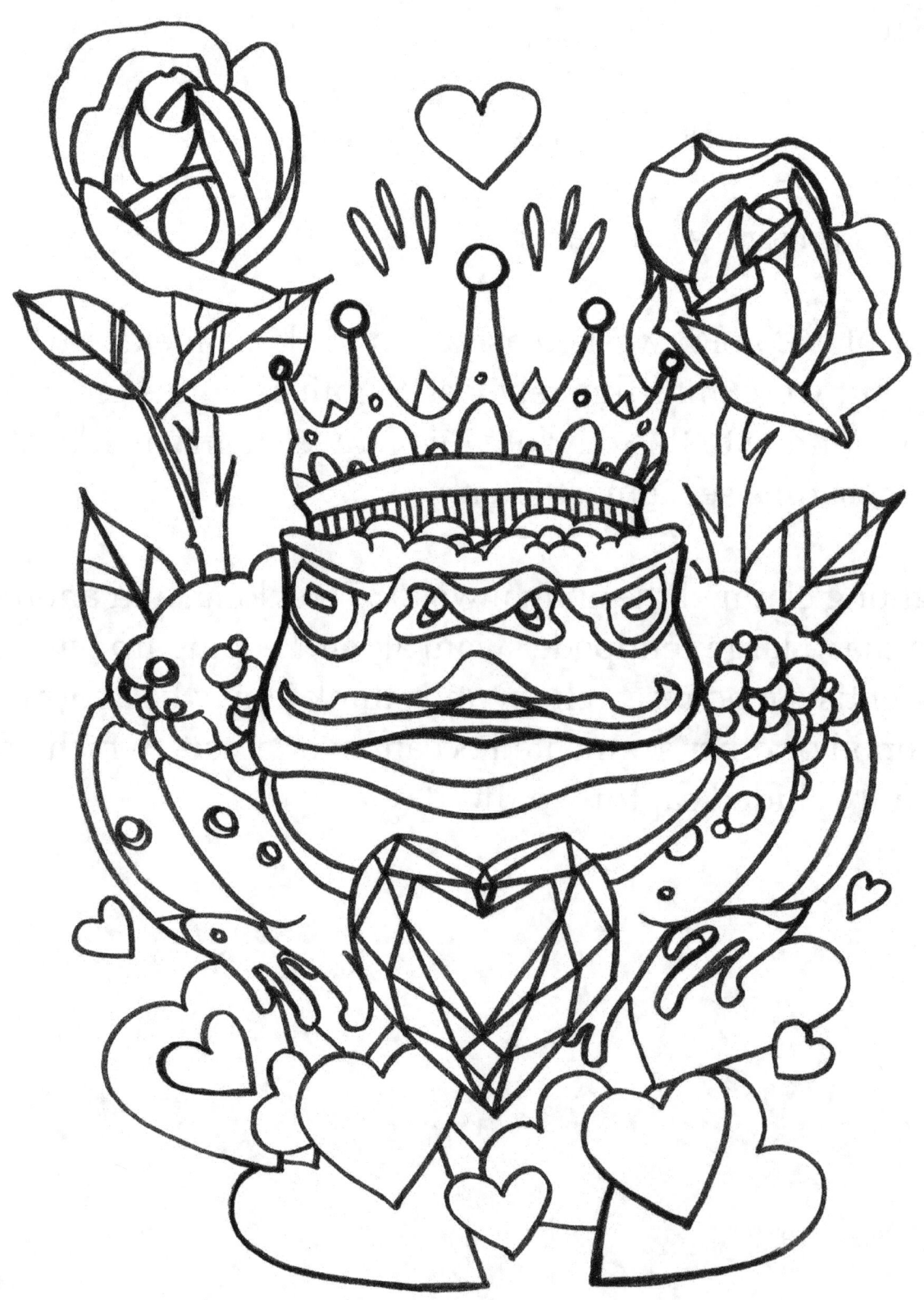

# The Frog Prince

In European and Chinese folktales, the frog prince is a temporarily humiliated Prince, a man who has been changed for some reason into a toad or frog. His punishment usually has to do with vanity or unkindness to others.

This curse can usually be lifted by a kiss from a maiden; in some cases true love is the only cure.

Since you can't catch warts from a frog or toad, there's no reason not to try kissing every single one of them, just in case.

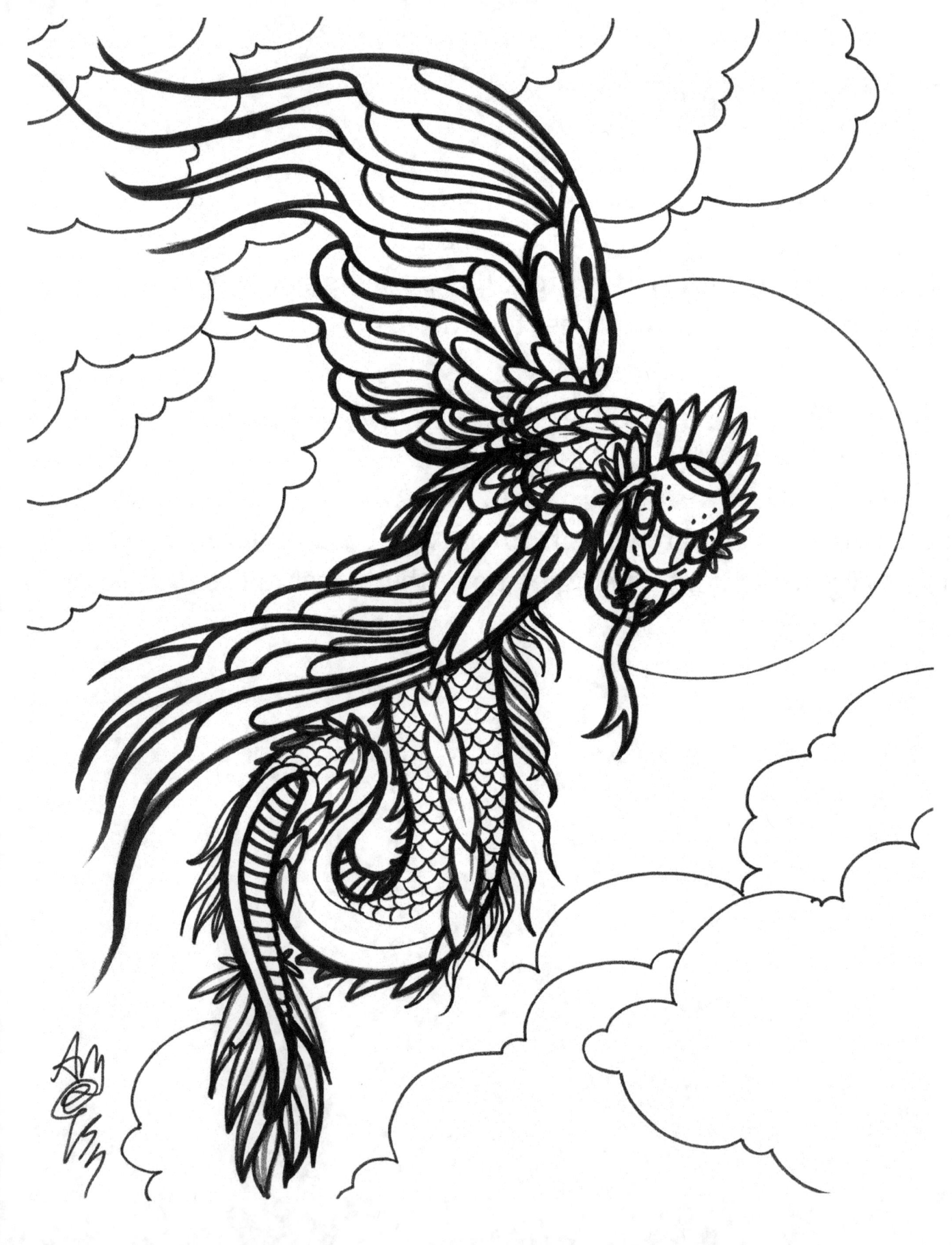

# Feathered Serpent

The feathered serpent, sometimes known as Quetzlcoatl, is a supernatural entity and/or deity, that is found in legend in South America and Central America.

It's said to be seen when natural forces are about to create a change; generally when a volcano may erupt, or an earthquake occur. It's often reported before a solar eclipse as well.

Since it is a serpent, it's associated with the earth; but it is covered in feathers and has wings, so it can fly too. It's seen as a connection between earth and daily affairs, and heaven and spiritual matters.

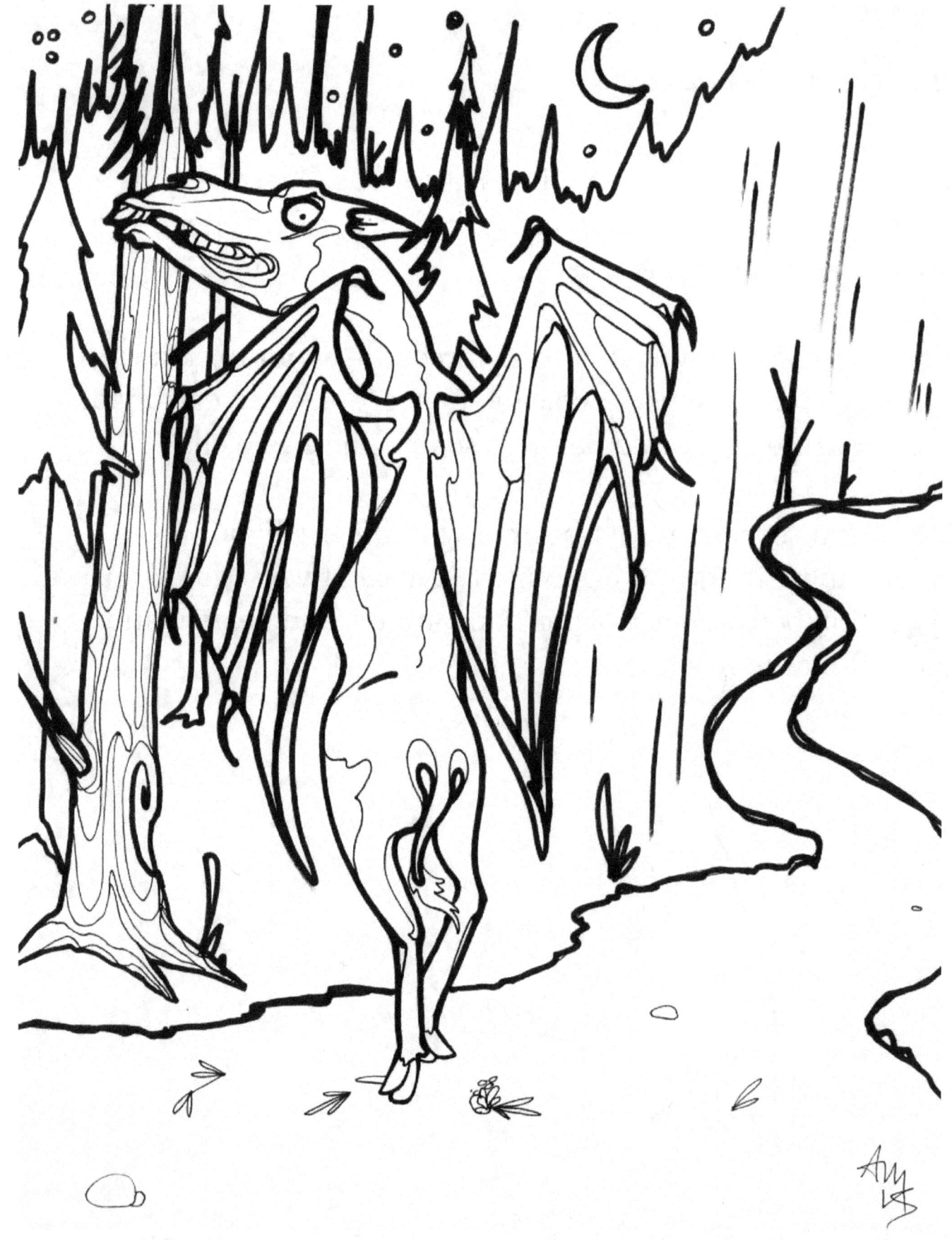

# Jersey Devil

I personally encountered the Jersey Devil, while taking a long solo hike through the Pine Barrens in New Jersey one evening. It was a grey, odd landscape. Upon coming around the bend of a trail, a *thing* ran past me, and across the trail.

It was the size of a small horse, with hind legs and with antlers. It had a horse's head, looked emaciated, and a deer's body with immense leathery wings.

I turned and ran back toward my original destination at full speed. I waited until the next day, at daylight, to hike past that point, of course accompanied by others. I noticed clear deer tracks in the dirt, with only two feet. . .

The Jersey Devil is a cryptid, a type of giant bat-deer, and alternately the evil deformed child of a satanic witch. Nobody knows its actual origins, but stories in the area are common. It's one of the few creatures in this book I have seen with my own eyes.

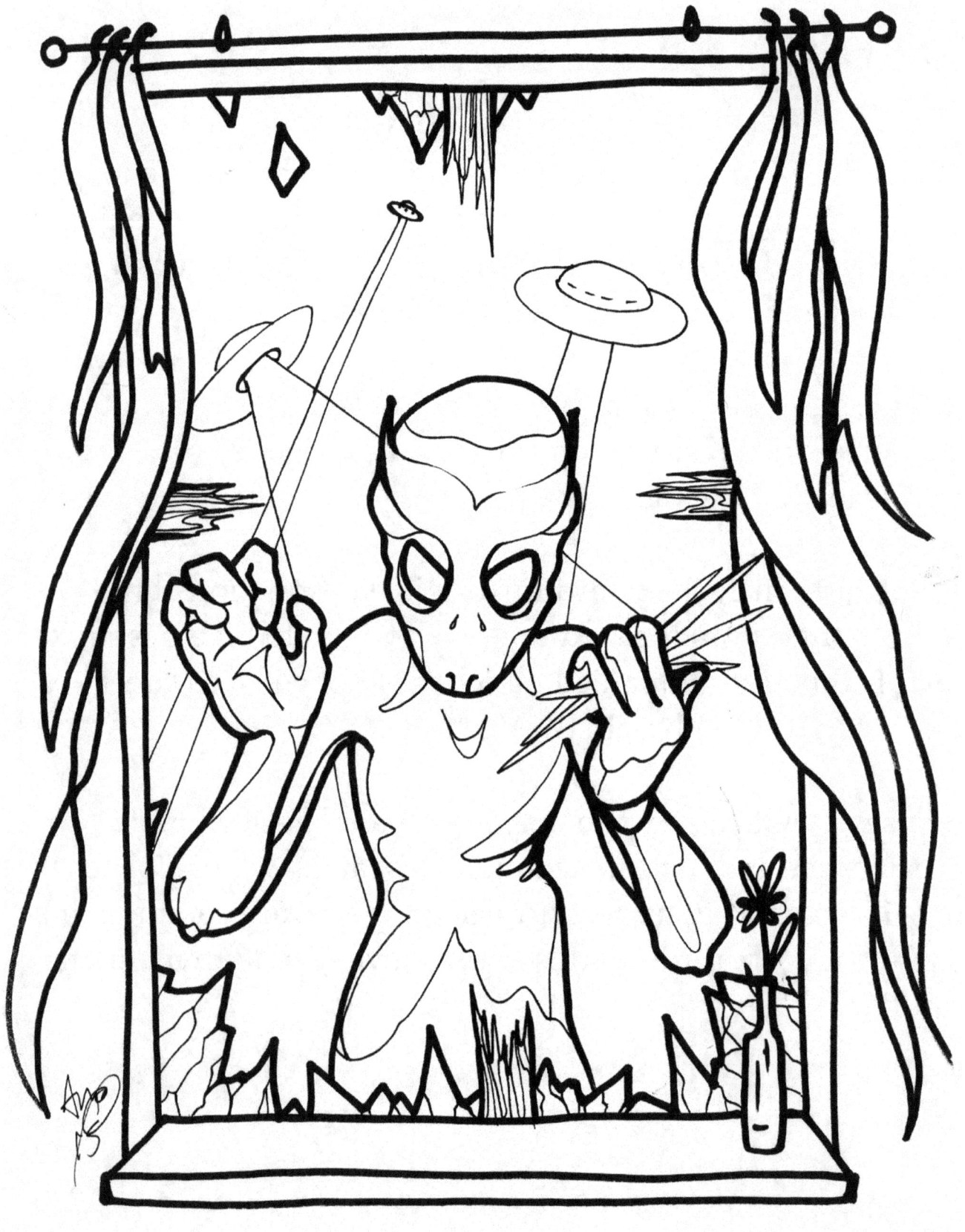

# Greys

When people talk about having encountered alien life, they're usually referring to the Greys. Simply put, they are the most commonly seen alien in all urban legend and all myth. They're usually described as small, with huge dark eyes and no mouth or jaw.

While many encounter the Greys while traveling, or are abducted from highways or roads, some people report home invasions by them. Greys will walk into the bedrooms of these abductees, snatch them and perform bizarre and inexplicable experiments on them.

Often the victims cannot remember quite clearly what's happened to them, they only know that they are missing an entire night or a day's worth of time.

There is no known way to fend off the Greys.

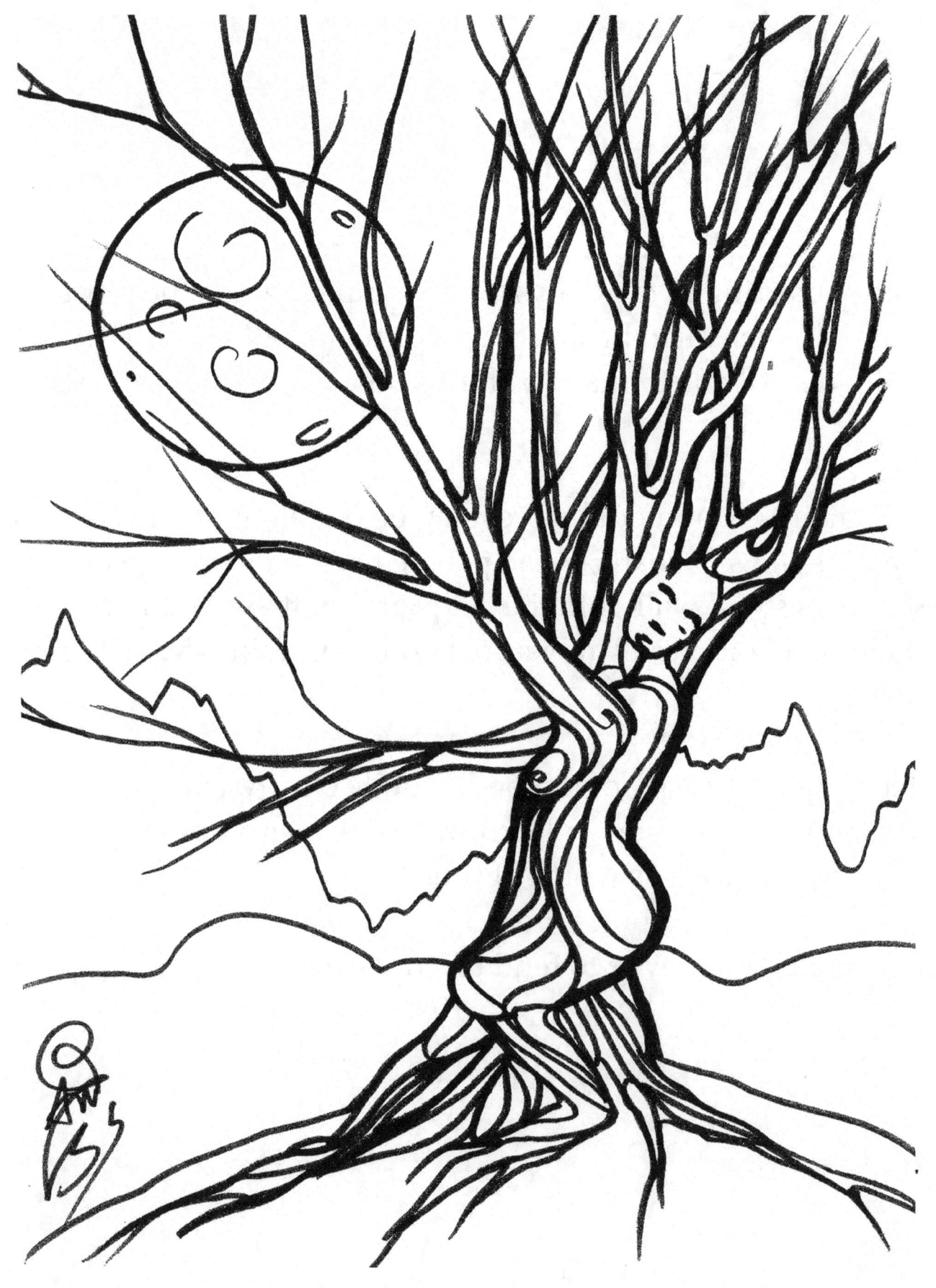

# Askafroa

The Askafroa is the "wife of the ash tree," a spirit noted by Germanic people that lives in the forest, that sleeps inside the trees. If disturbed, she may cause bad luck for any building nearly; and it has been also said to occasionally attack those who chop wood in the deep forest.

Askafroas are similar to Dryads in myth, but people who live near the dark forests believe them to be a real, always taking steps to make sure not to disturb the groves they inhabit.

It's common knowledge that if any Askafroa is malicious, sacrificial offerings will sate them. Animal, or human.

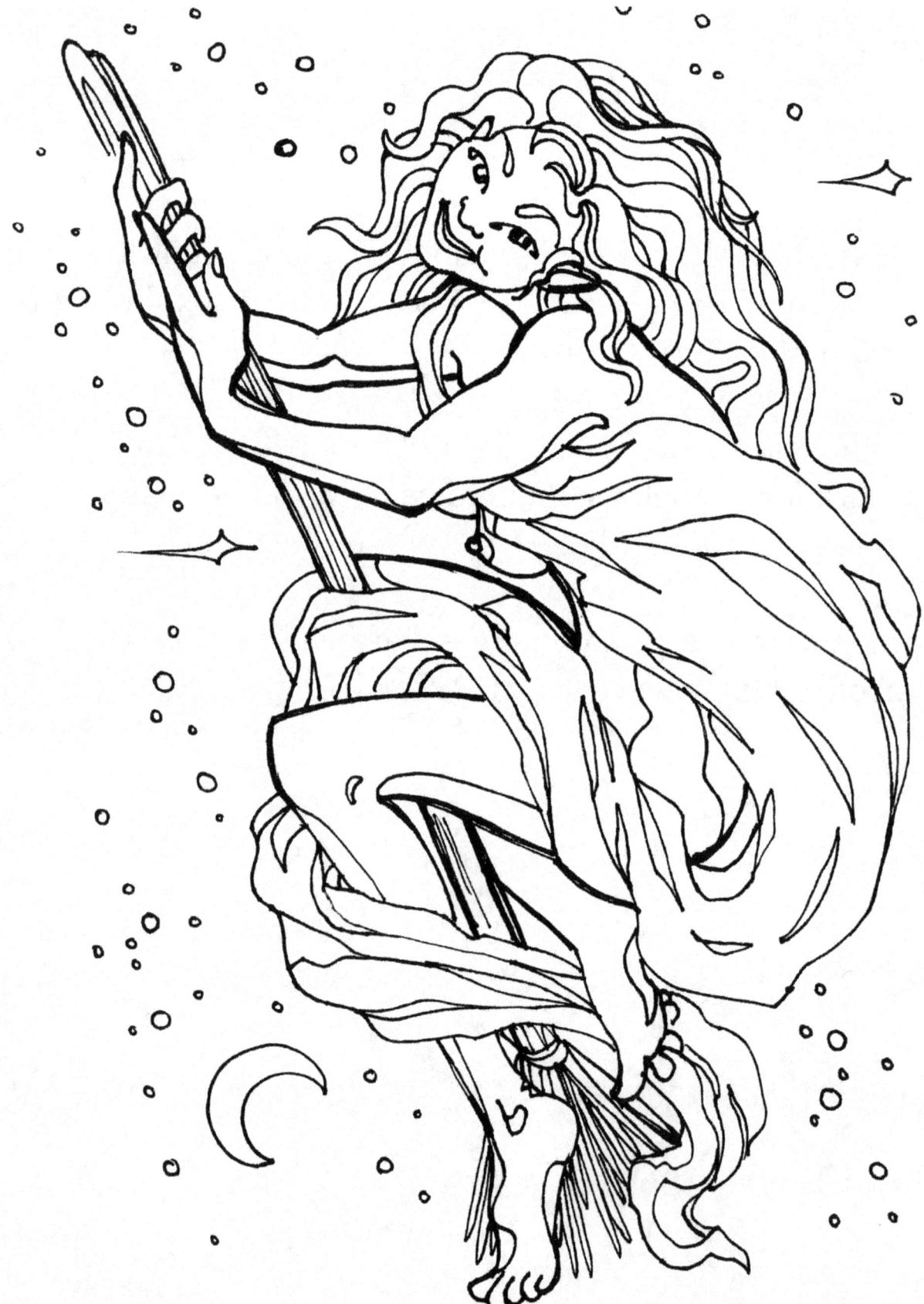

# Witch

In Italy and Spain, witches were considered to be so vile that they should be burned. Some pastimes of these medieval witches included having sex with the devil, greasing themselves with infant's fat, cursing livestock, and of course, flying- with or without a broomstick.

This classic witch comes from catholic myth, and many real people were killed during the inquisition by the religious authorities, after being forced to confess to being witches.

The witch was a frightening creature to people at that time, as they were thought to be able to kill with a word, curse women to miscarry, and kill livestock from a distance… although nowadays witches are usually content to make herbal teas and play around with crystals.

In some places witches are still believed to be real, and are attacked or murdered by local people.

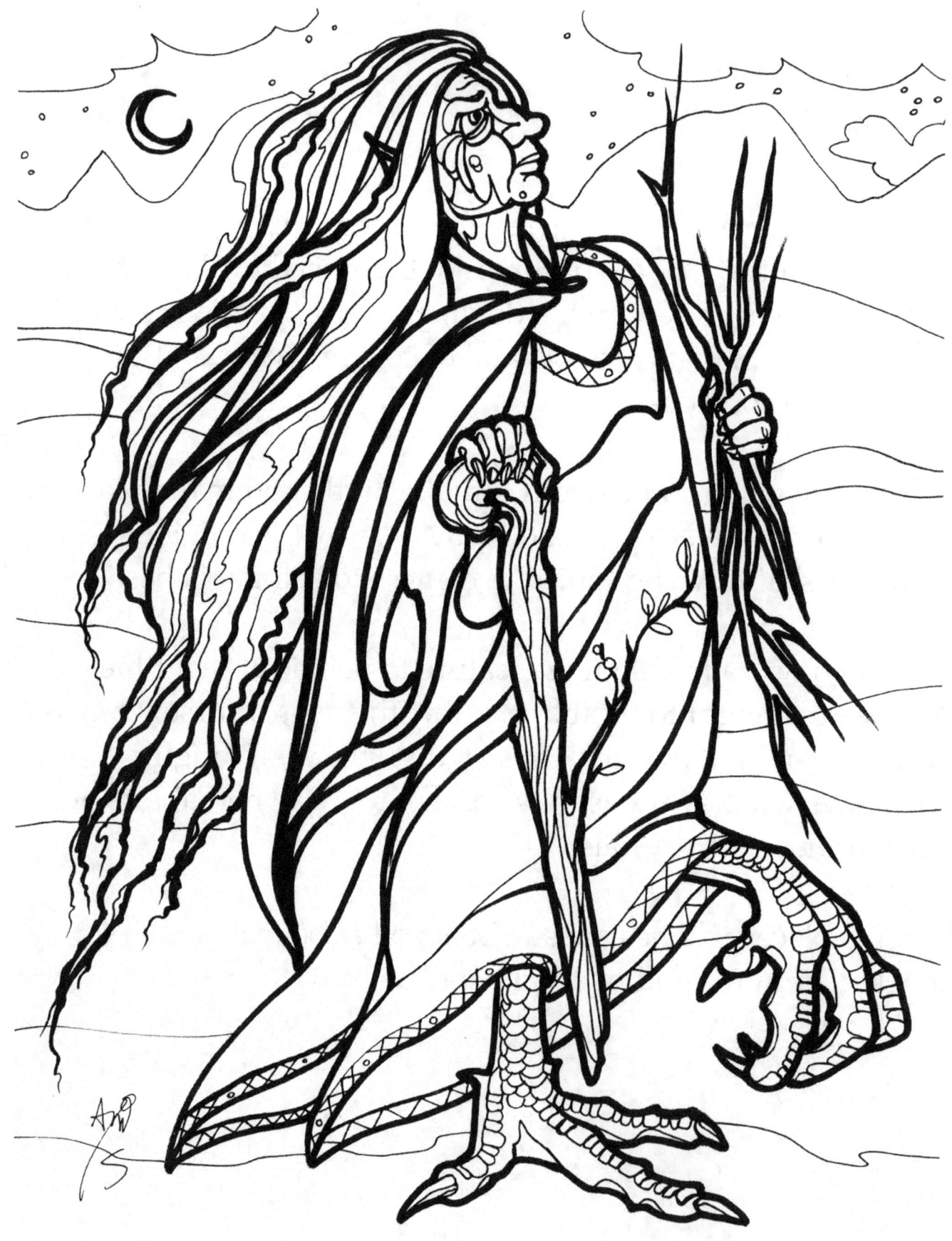

# Baba Yaga

Baba Yaga is a Russian and Siberian mythological creature. She's an old hag who tries to con travelers into staying with her.

She can be discovered by looking at her feet, as she has the feet of a giant chicken instead of human feet.

If a traveler doesn't realize he's agreed to stay with Baba Yaga, she will cook and eat him.

It's said that her cottage is enchanted and time passes differently there. It, too, has the legs and feet of a chicken.

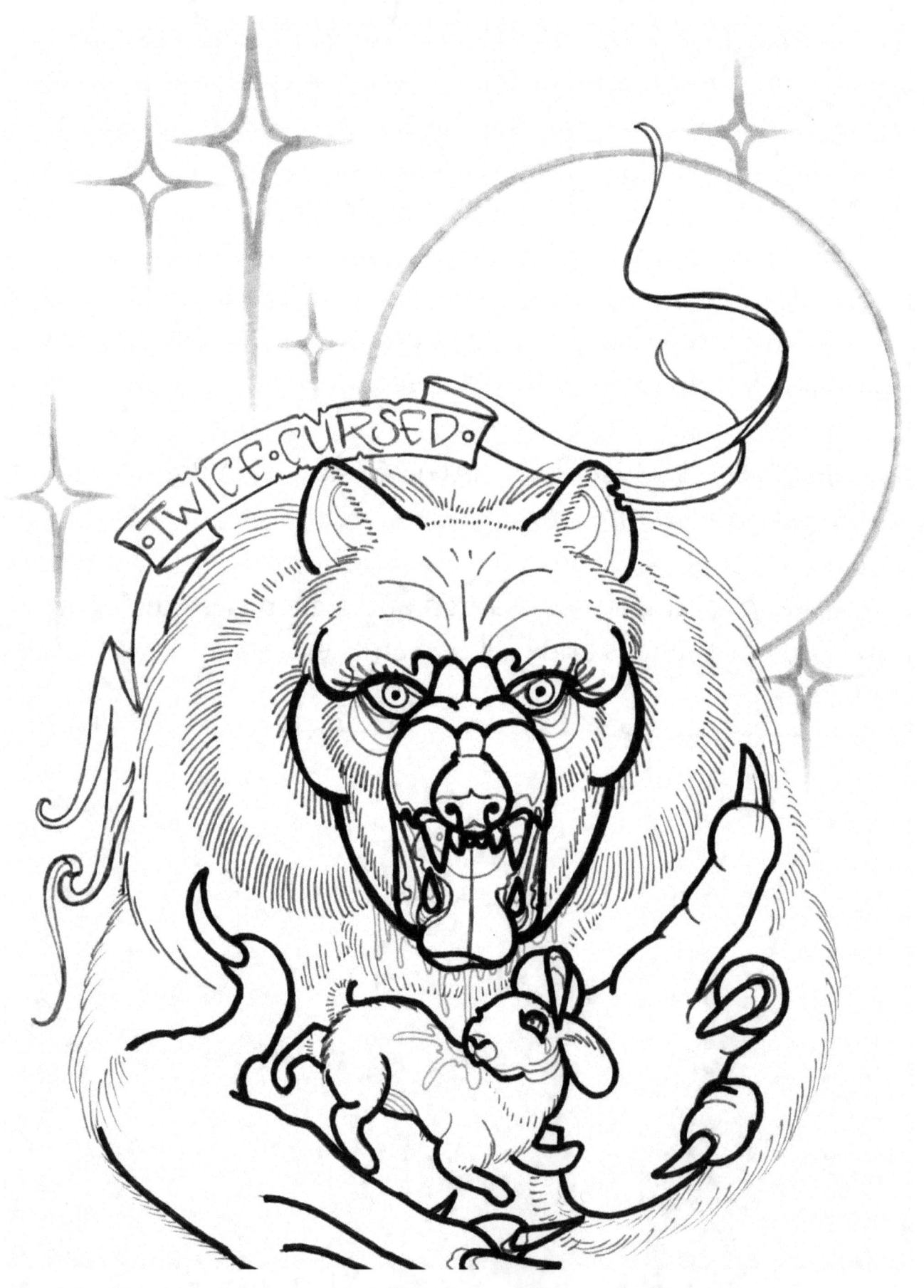

# Werewolf

The Werewolf is well-known in popular culture and horror movies. Usually portrayed as a tragic, cursed and noble man who is dragged down into his animal nature, the modern werewolf has little in common with the old eastern European myth surrounding these creatures.

In old times, any wolf or wolf-like creature killed during the gibbous moon could become a Werewolf, a creature intelligent enough to pass for a human being. Even further east, in Russia and far eastern Europe, Werewolves were human beings who chose the curse. They were people who were aggressive and violent, murderers or the old-time equivalent of serial killers.

A common thread in these myths is that Werewolves do not like to stay in one place for long, but prefer to travel or live nomadically. They change to their most violent, animalistic form with the full moon. Burning or destroying their fur-skin would then kill them or cure them, depending on which myth you're reading. Recognizing a Werewolf involves looking under its tongue (while in human form) and finding bristles there. Other signs include a unibrow, curved fingernails, and low-set ears.

In most myths about Werewolves, silver is mentioned as a weakness, hence the popular conception of a "silver bullet." It was once believed that restraining a Werewolf and allowing it to become exhausted would cure it. In some areas of Hungary and Bulgaria, Wolfsbane or certain fungi are said to be cures. In parts of Germany, to call its "true name," its human name, three times will cure it.

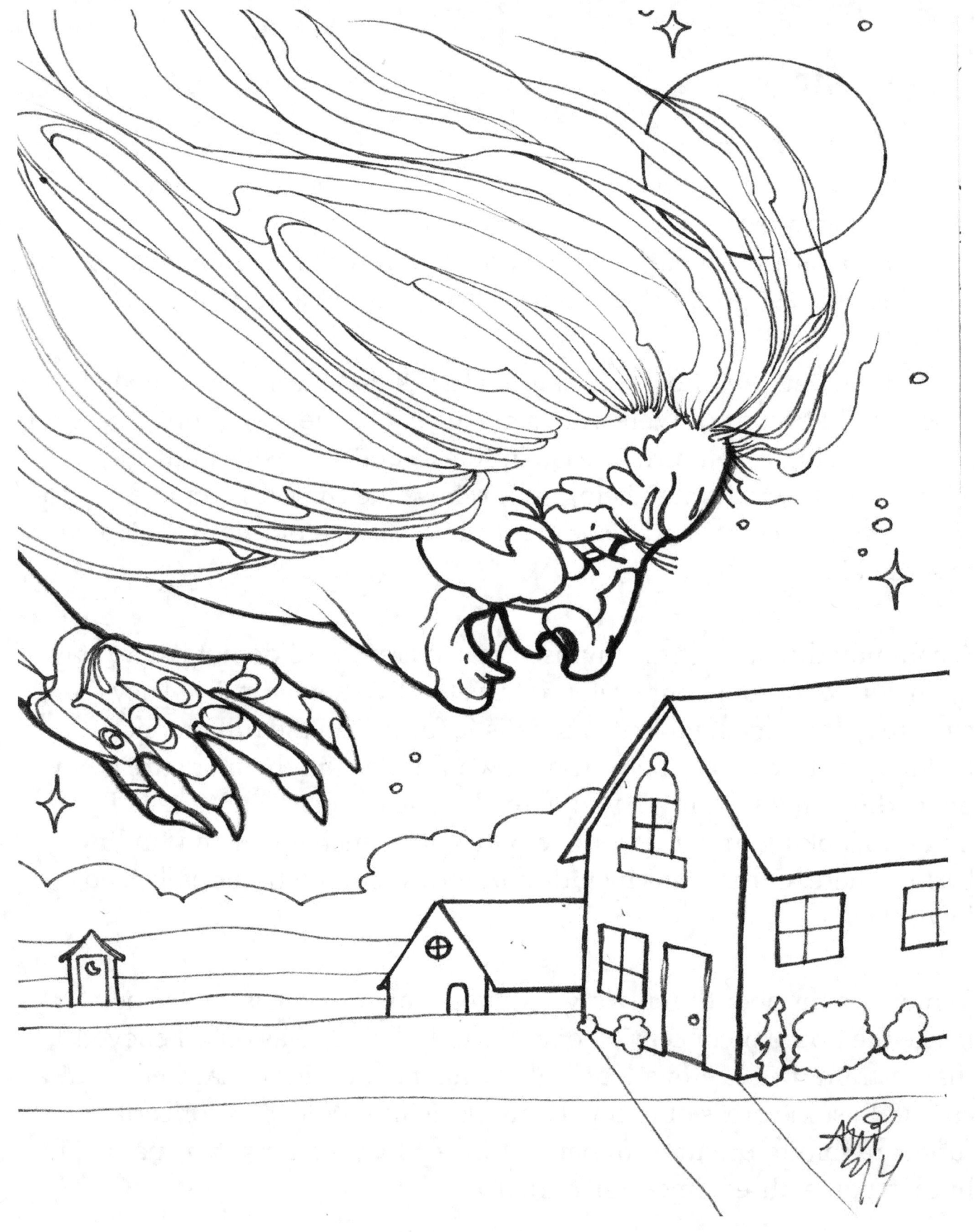

# Banshee

I have a personal experience with the Banshee. Half of my family is originally Cork County Irish. My great grandmother was in her 80s when she died at home, after a long battle with liver failure. In the nights before she died, my cousin claimed to have heard the wind screaming like a woman, right outside their windows; our family has stories going generations back of the Banshee attending deaths.

The Banshee wails to announce death, as she is a messenger. Few people actually see her; if they do, it is an omen they will die suddenly. Some families have their own Banshee, who follows them from generation to generation. Others simply encounter the Banshee occasionally.

She is usually dressed in white or grey shrouds and may appear, flying outside an upper-story window, or from the trees in a nearby woods.

There is no way to defeat or avoid the Banshee. However, if you see a comb on the ground, do not pick it up! Banshees comb their long hair and will drop their comb to the ground, then curse the person who claims it.

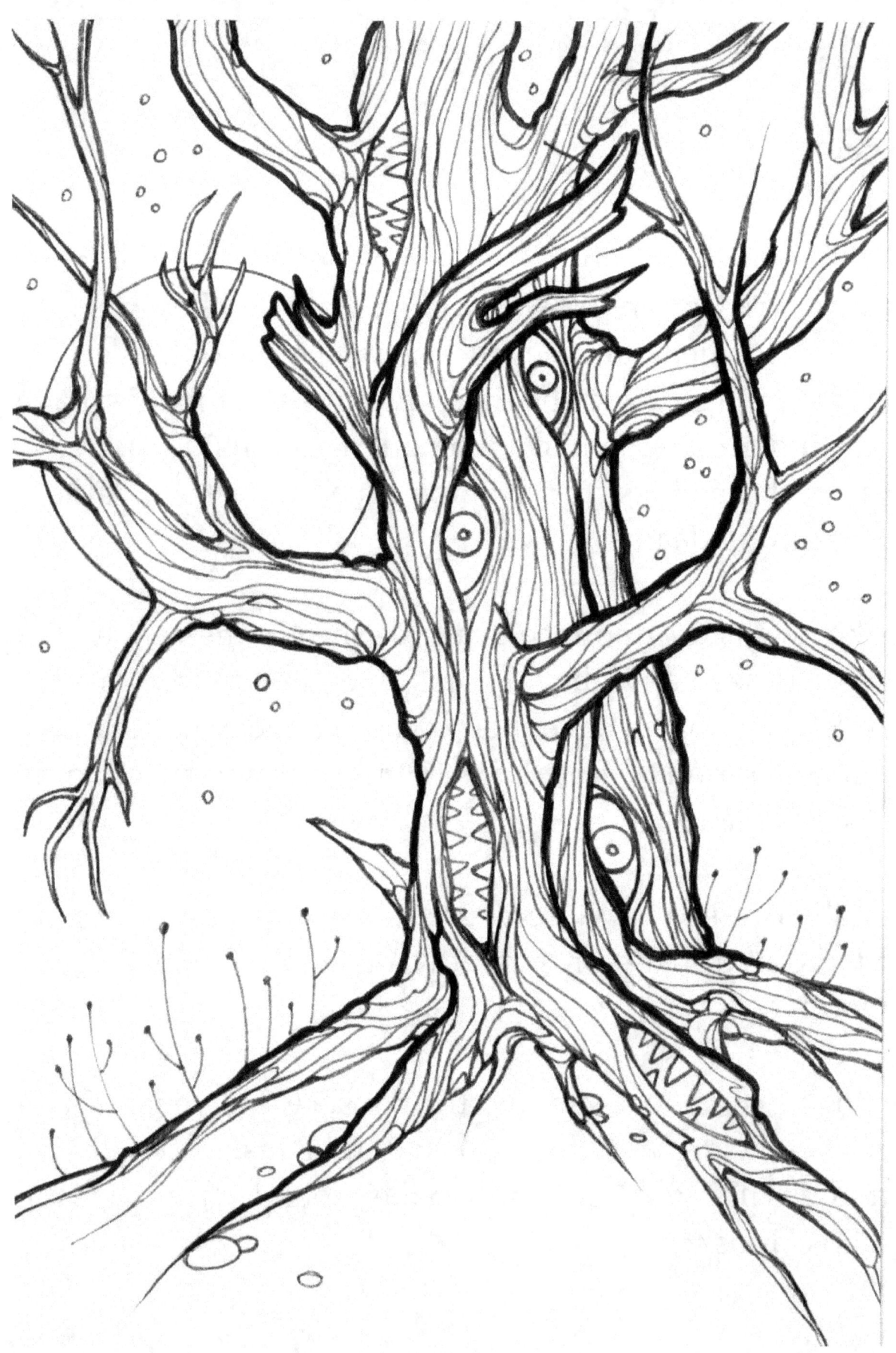

# Ya te Veo

The Ya te Veo is a cryptid from Madagascar. It's one of the few botanical cryptids in existence.

The Ya te Veo is a man-eater. It has branches which it can move, to clutch and grab. It has eyes and mouths concealed in its bark, it waits until its victims are close, then grabs and devours them.

Translated to English, Ya te Veo means *"I see you."*

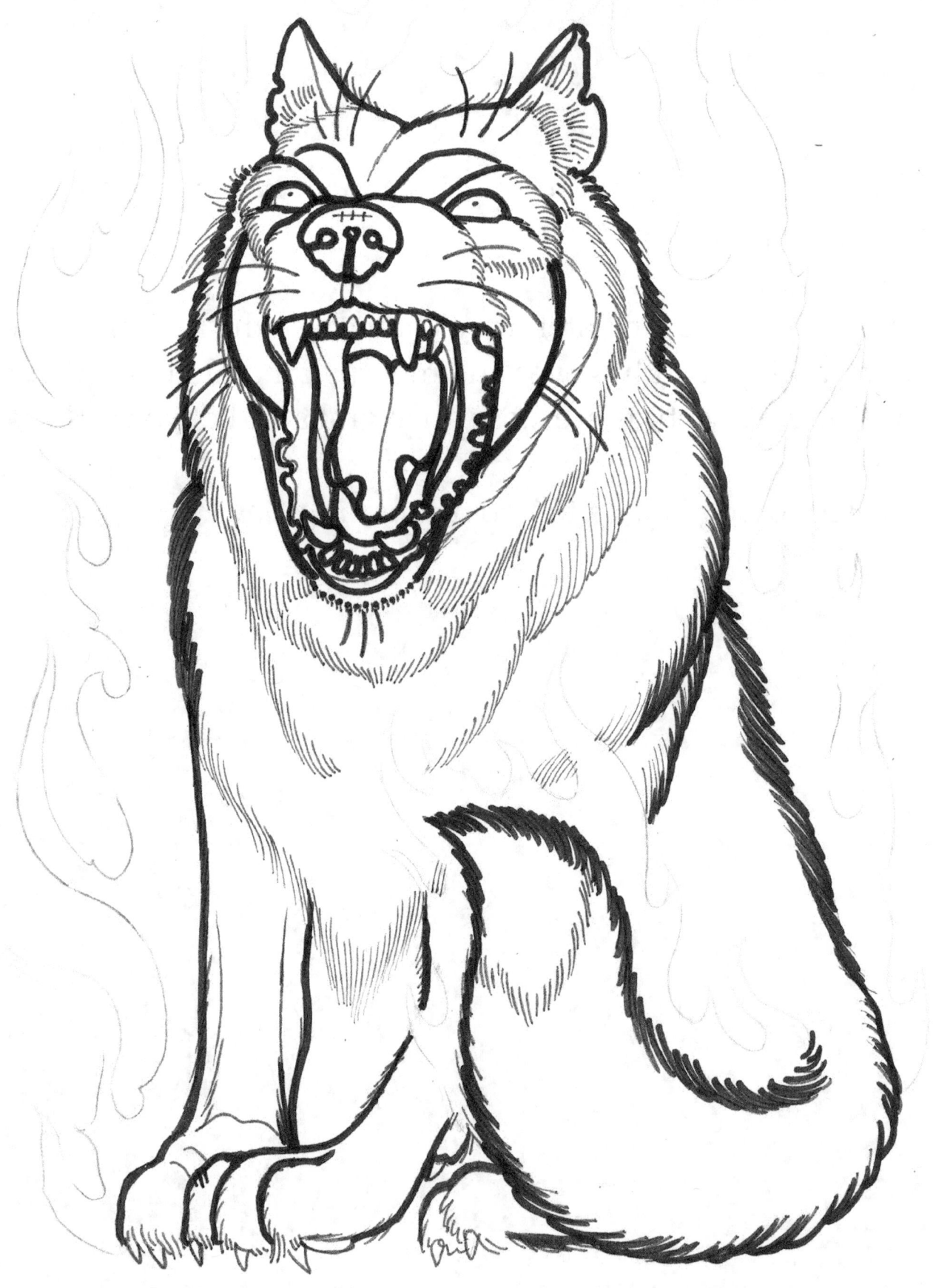

# Black Shuck

Black Shuck is a dark hound from the British Isles. He's said to follow people late at night, stalking them and terrifying them with his red eyes and glowing green aura. Some say that seeing this black dog is an omen of death, that it's a spirit informing the person they will soon die. Others claim that the Black Shuck is protecting those who have seen him against some worse fate, interfering in accidents, muggings, and ambushes.

The Black Shuck has been a part of folklore in the area since at least the 1500s. Early accounts its appearance were printed at that time, claiming it had entered a church and attacked the priest. Other tales seem related to werewolves, tales of the Black Shuck being injured and then a person in the area being found with the same injuries.

The Black Shuck is usually considered unnatural, a ghost or spirit.

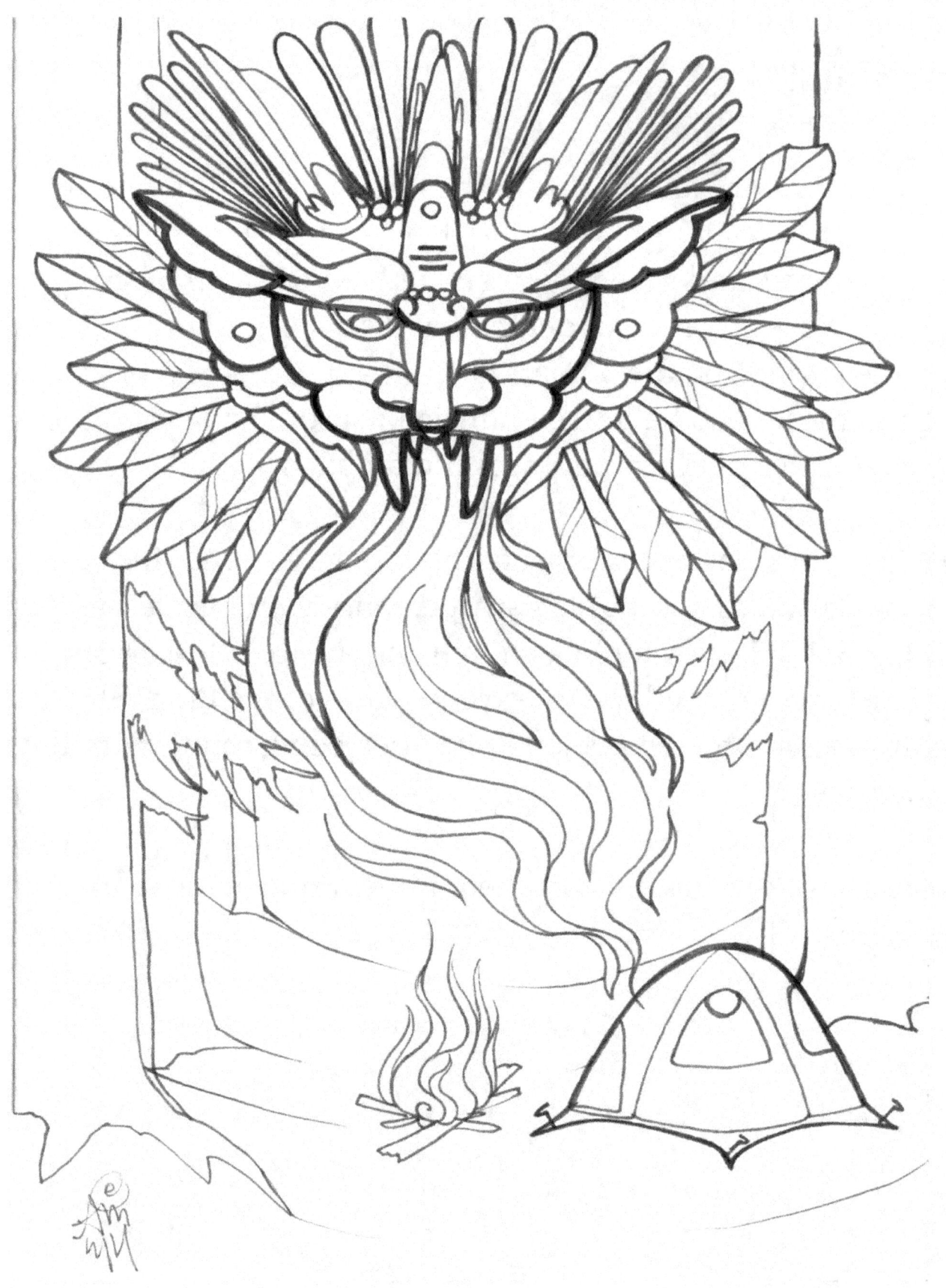

# Wendigo

In North American mythology, the Wendigo is regarded as a forest spirit which can possess humans, if they indulge in cannibalism. This will cause them to become insatiable for human meat.

Later stories cast the Wendigo as a wind spirit which will lift a person into the air, forcing them to run faster and faster until their feet begin to burn from the friction, eventually burning them down to nothing. At this point, the victim becomes a Wendigo and will often come back to seize his friends or family in the same way.

In the coniferous forests of the Pacific Northwest, the sound of the wind in the tall trees can definitely sound at times like a human voice calling a name.

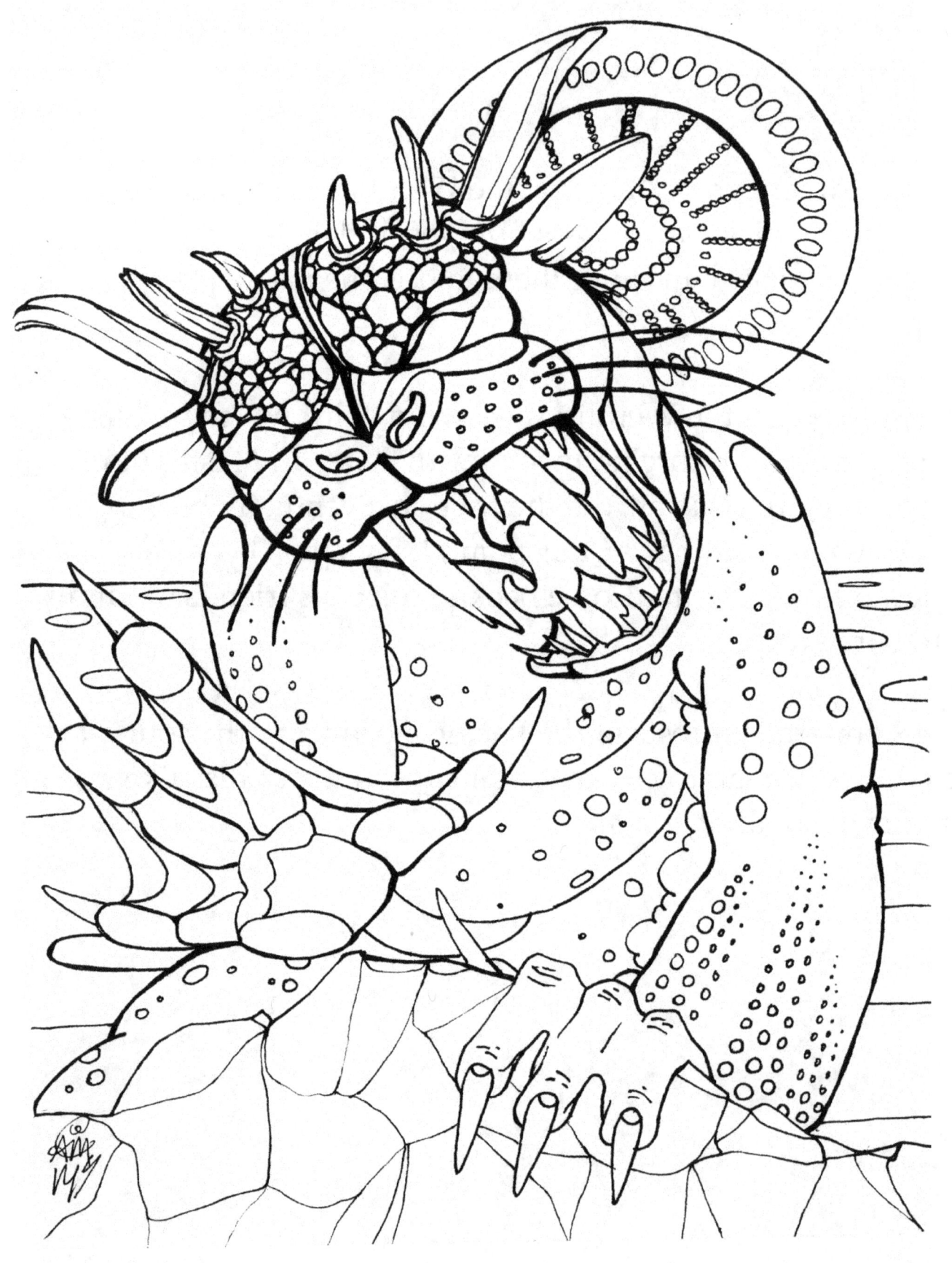

# The Bunyip

The Bunyip is a mythological creature from Australia. It's a water creature, living near lakes and rivers. Stories of the bunyip are thousands of years old.

They've been reported to attack people. The Bunyip swims expertly, walks upright, and kills prey by crushing or "hugging" it to death.

There are reports of the Bunyip dragging women into the river to drown them as they do laundry. The Bunyip is not like a person or a supernatural being. It's simply a mythological animal, more than likely a predator.

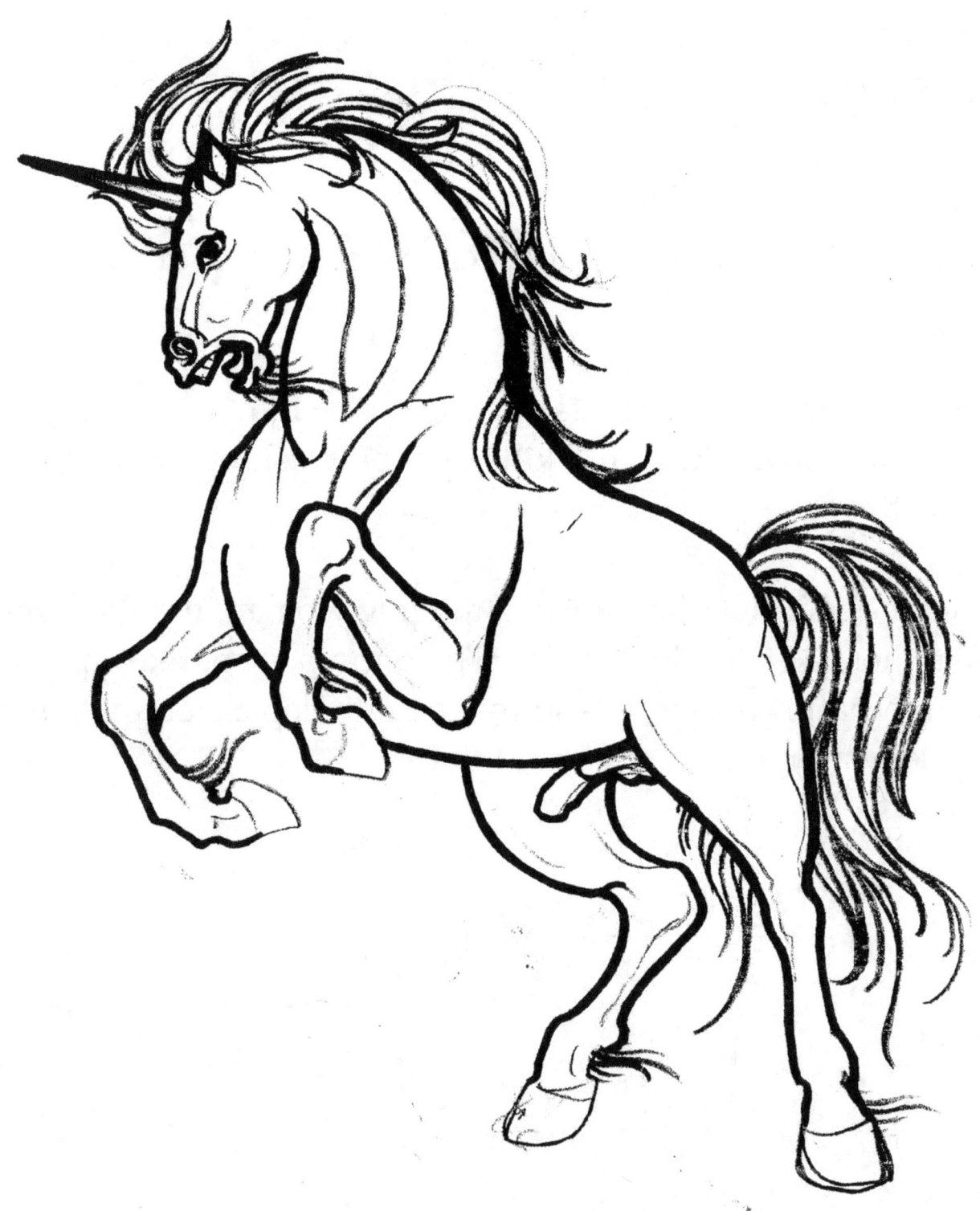

# Unicorn

Unicorns have roots in Greek mythology, and were referred to in texts during the Middle Ages.

It has long been believed that they were discovered in India during the 6$^{th}$ century. Some people believe them to be a symbol of purity and it's commonly known that they'll only allow pure young girls to pet them.

In European tapestries, they are hunted using virgins as bait.

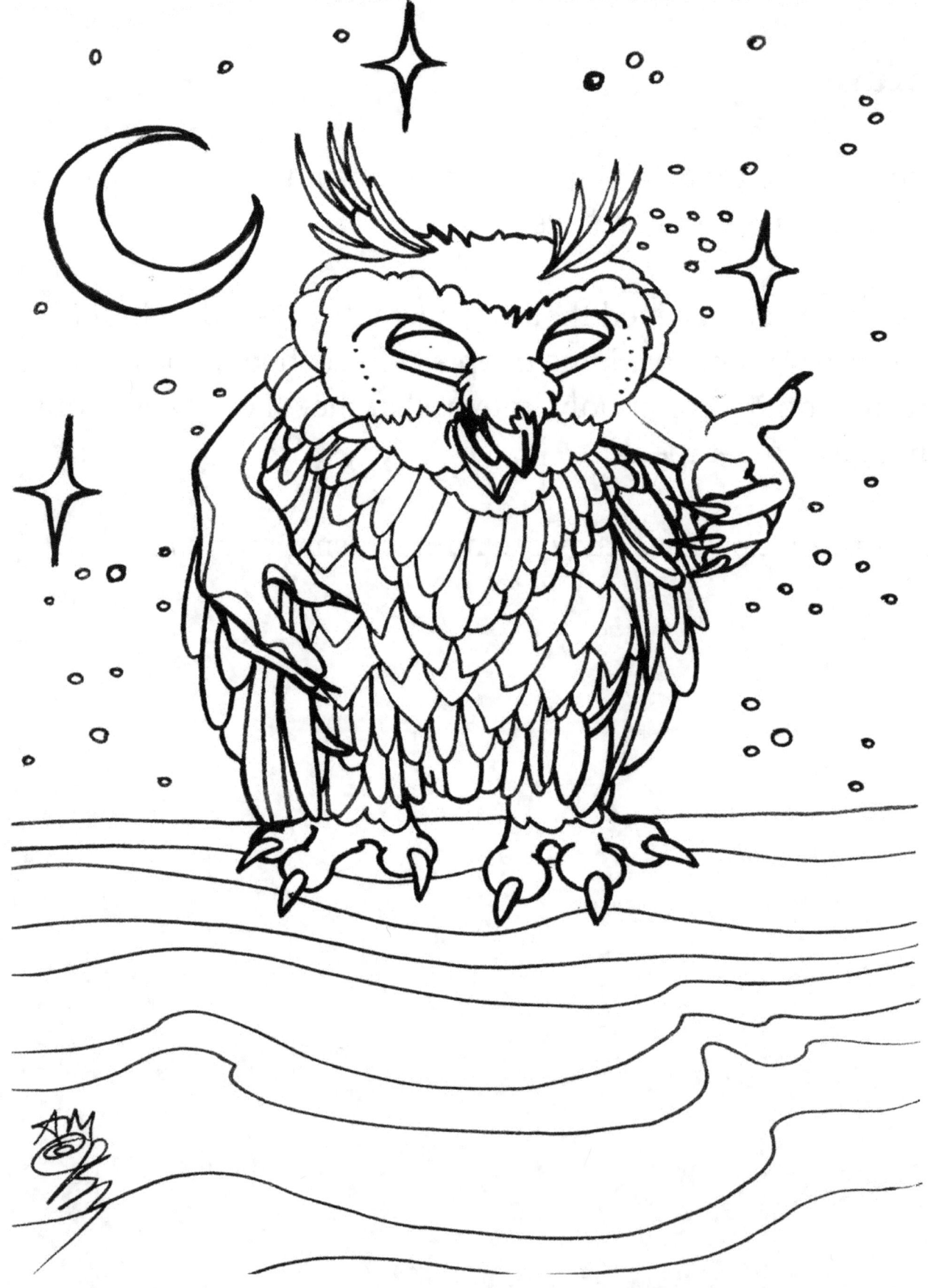

# Chickcharney

The Chickcharney is a cryptid that comes from urban legends in the Bahamas. It's a small creature, only a few feet tall, and appears at night along the roads.

While the Chickcharney looks something like an owl, it also has human hands and eyes. It's covered in feathers, as well as fur. In the urban legends, it may ask for a ride, a drink of water, or simply stand alongside a traveler's path.

If the traveler treats it kindly, it will give them good luck on their journey. If they treat it poorly, their journey will have bad luck, and many obstacles.

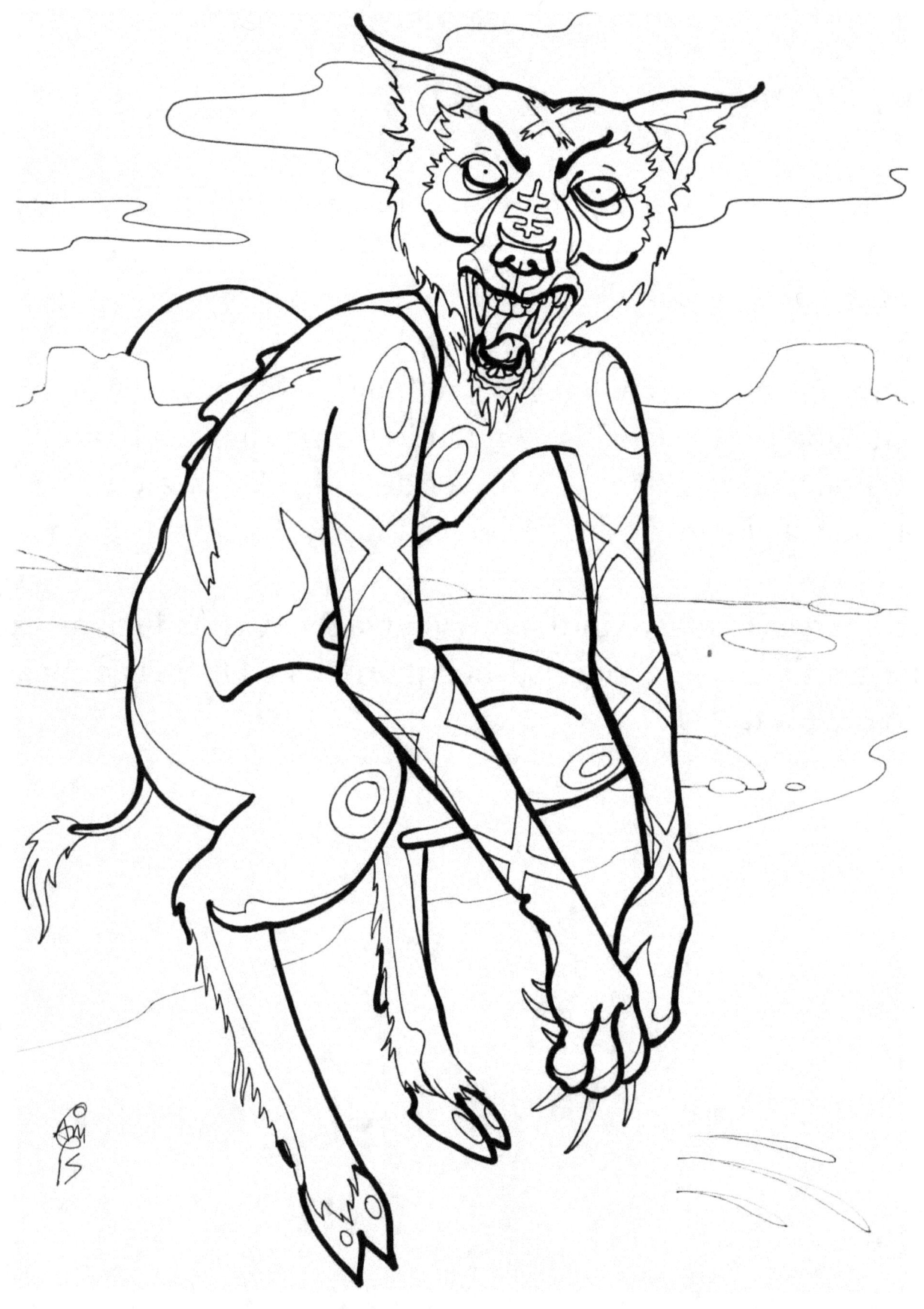

# Skin-walker

Skin-walkers are traditionally Navajo shamans who have gone down the dark path. They've indulged in human sacrifice or brutality in order to gain more power. This transforms them into something not-human, a shapeshifter who can only be a thing whose skin is stolen.

Most often they can be seen in coyote/human form or as deer men. They may use mimicry to attract people into the woods to find new skin. If given such an opportunity, there's a good chance they will interact with others in the form that person. Since Skin-walkers abandoned their humanity, they are socially inapt and unable to hold conversations.

The Navajo do not speak of them, believing it may draw their attention. According to urban legend, most drugs will kill them, and gold dust will chase them from the body they're inhabiting.

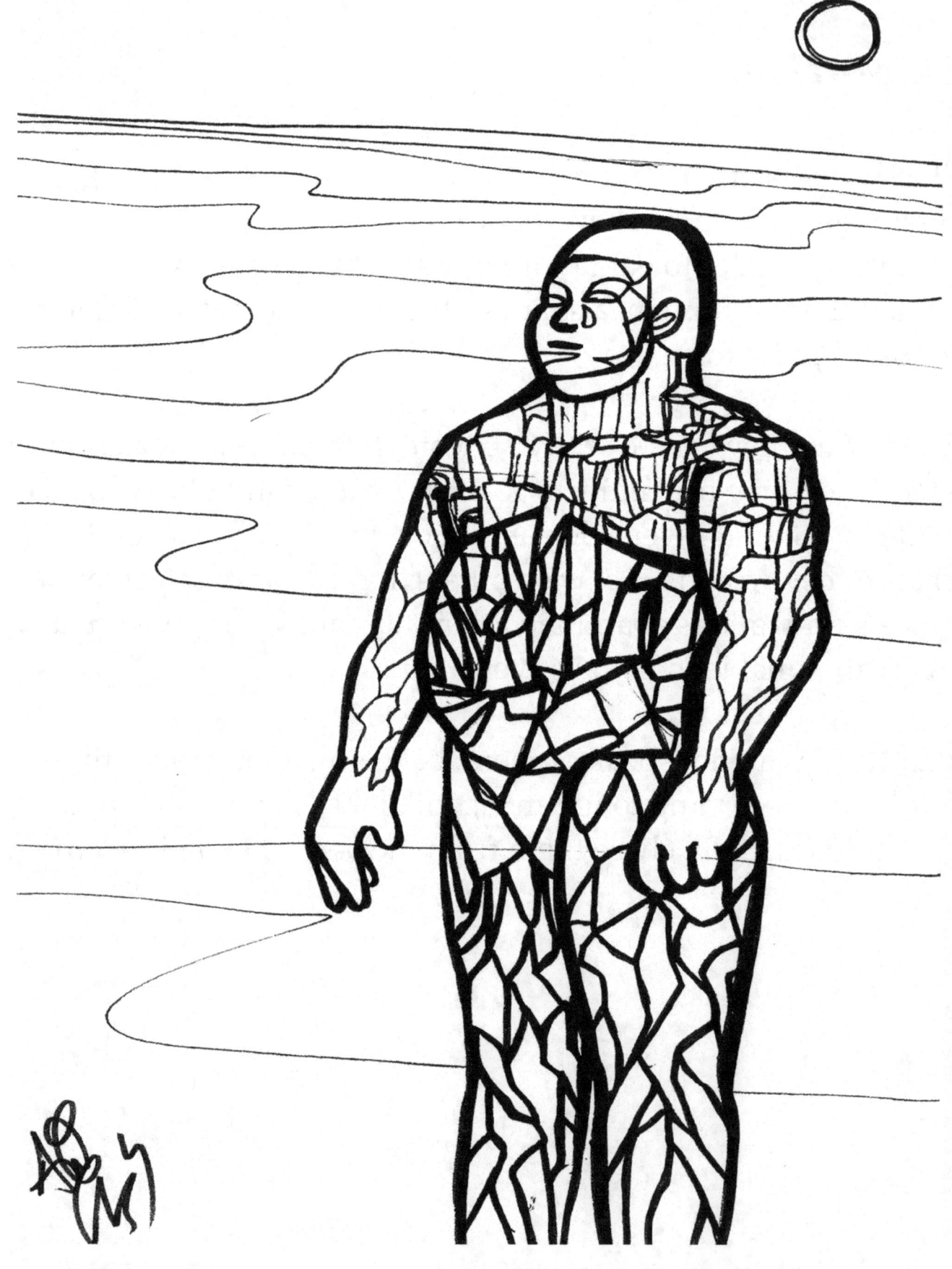

# Golem

A Golem is a Jewish legend; made of clay, stone, or stuffing, it's an inanimate creature that is animated by writing a special word or phrase on a scroll and placing it into its mouth. This paper contains the creature's instructions, hence these directions must be worded carefully, as the golem has no mind and will follow them to the letter.

Golems sometimes become violent, and must be stopped. In some cases even its creator cannot stop it. The only way to stop a Golem is by removing the paper scroll, which will cause it to become inanimate again. Using reflections in mirrors or water may confuse the Golem if necessary.

Most Golems are said to be made of stone or clay, but modern legends include plastic, stuffed animals, and other items and materials.

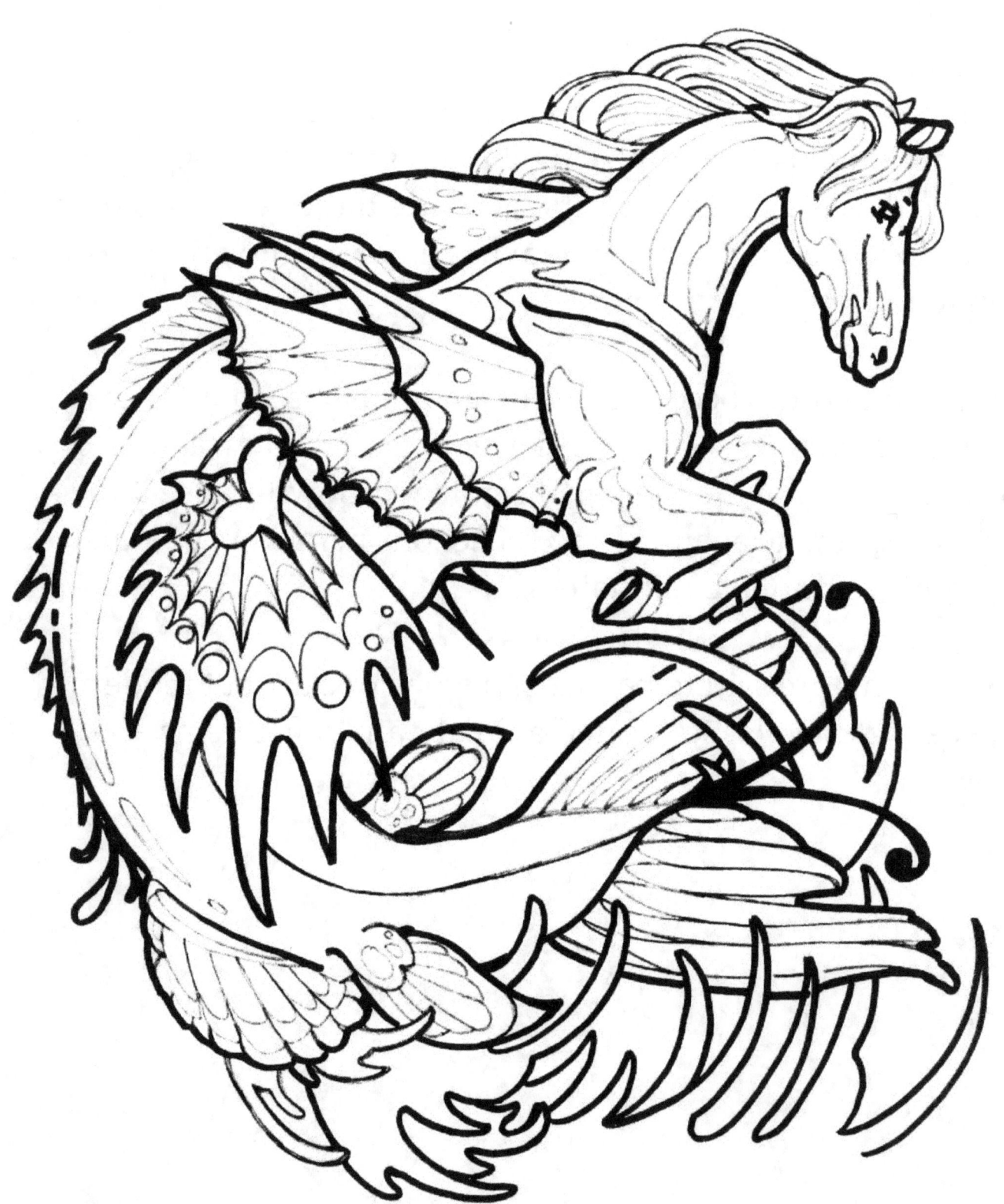

# Kelpie

Kelpies look like a normal horse in front- usually beautiful, healthy horses.

Their fur is soft and silky like a seal's, their skin smooth and soft but very cold to the touch.

The kelpie pretends to be a lost horse, walking along the edge of the surf. Since horses are valuable and an unclaimed horse is tempting, many will approach it to take it in. Instead, the kelpie lures the person to touch it. The hand will become stuck fast, and the kelpie will immediately turn into the deeps, dragging the person down into the water and drowning them.

In some myths the kelpie encourages the person to ride it, to get up on its back. Then it races into the ocean, drowning the person and devouring them, leaving the heart and liver.

Kelpies spend most of their time just under the surface, only their eyes and nose breaking the surface, as they wait for someone to come along and become the next victim.

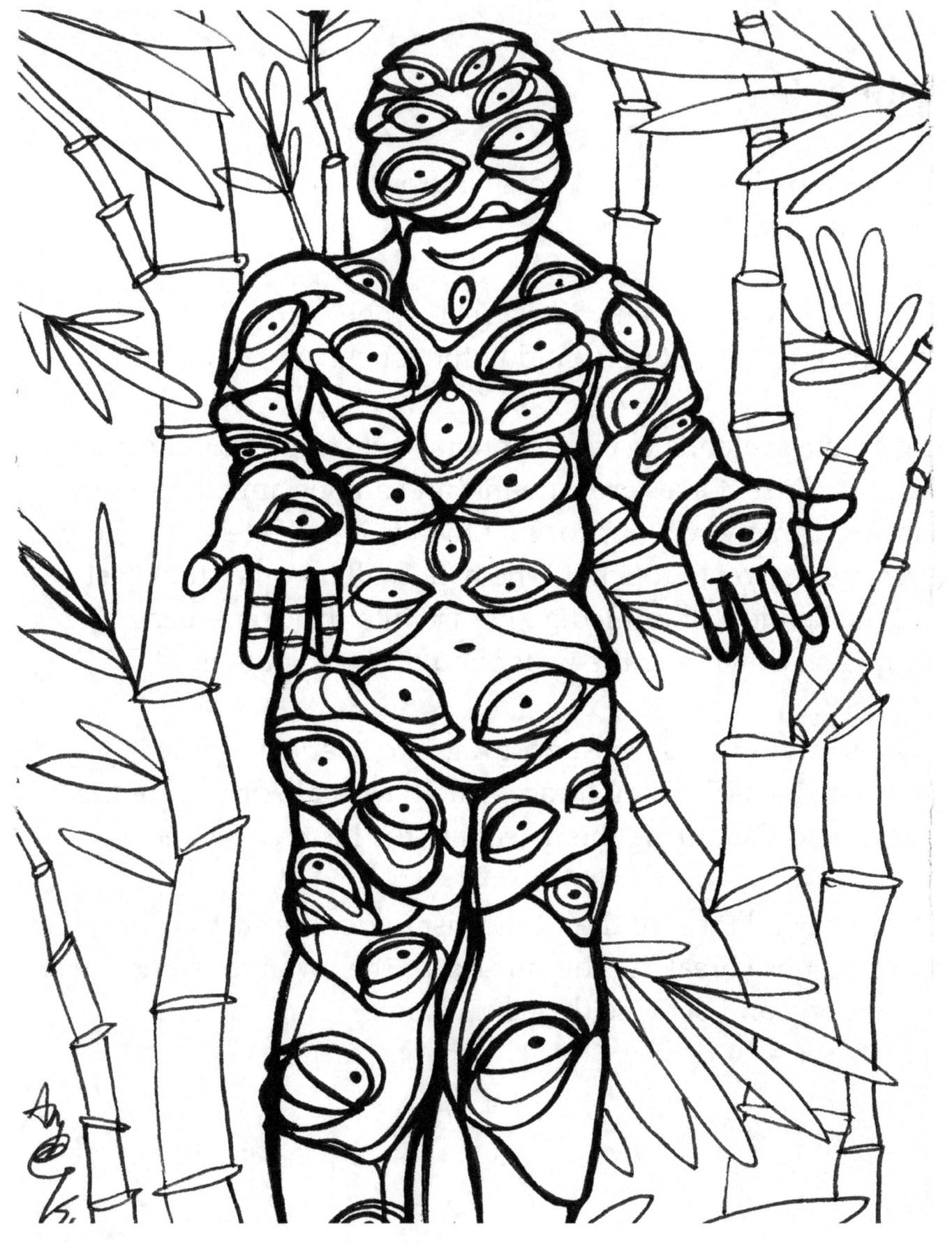

# Hyakume

Hyakume are reported in Japan. They're vaguely humanoid, but appear as a lumpy mass of flesh covered in eyes. When their eyes are closed, they resemble a lump of flesh; when their eyes are open and the Hyakume is awake, it's an eerie sight.

Hyakume live in old temples and cemeteries, crypts, and altars. They're said to guard against those who would steal the offerings left there.

Their many eyes make it impossible for them to stand the daylight, so they only emerge at night. They spend the day with all eyes closed, hiding in the shadows under buildings or rocks. At night they roam the area, startling visitors and attacking would-be thieves.

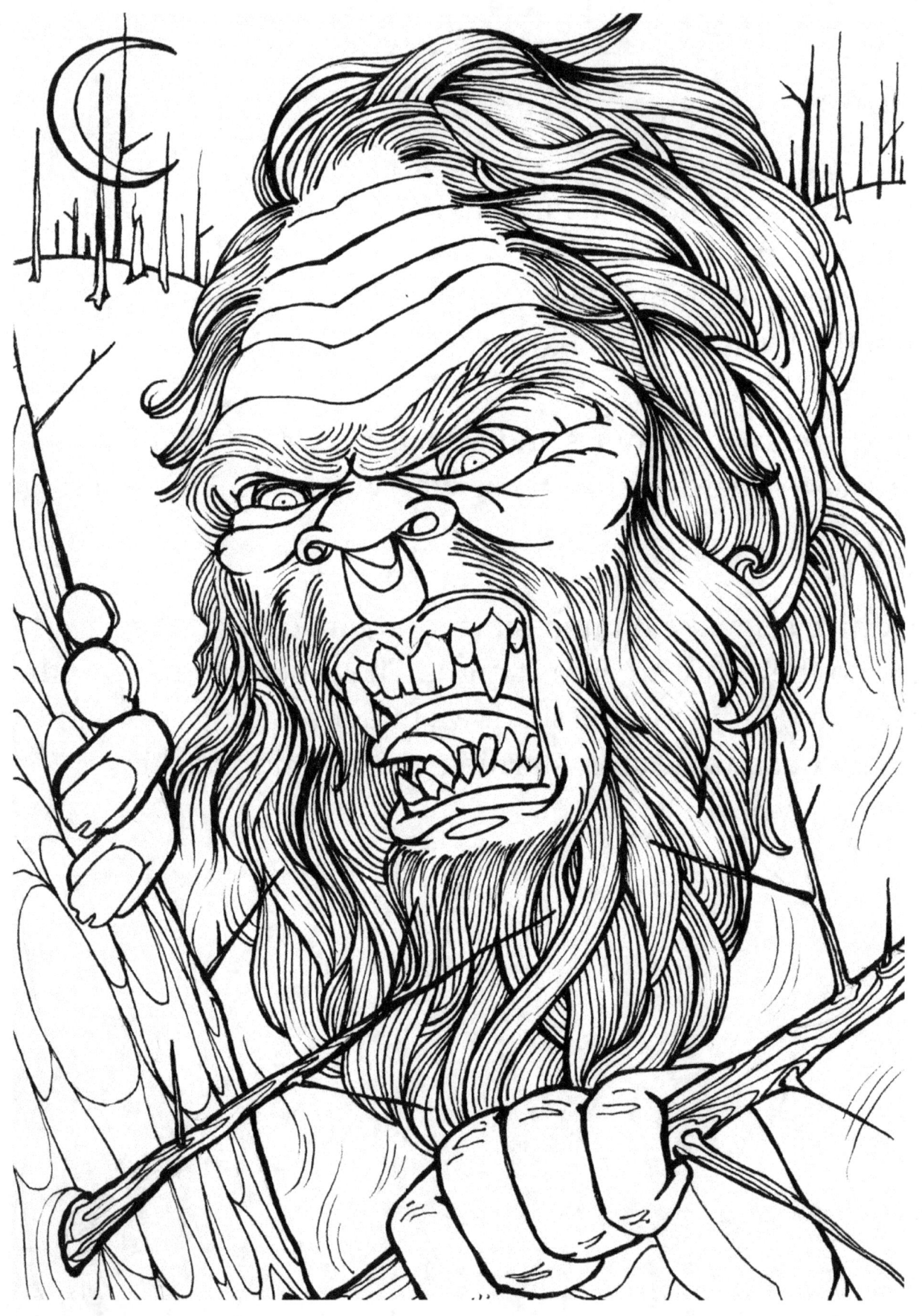

# Sasquatch

I once knew a person who heard a Sasquatch shouting and bellowing at night, out on a lonely lake. He described the experience in detail, yet I didn't believe him.

A few years later, I was camping in the deep woods in the north half of the Siuslaw forest in Oregon by myself. I had walked a day from every marked trail and camping area, to reach the thicker woods. At three in the morning I awoke to a deep thumping sound, from the middle distance.

The only animals there large enough to make such a noise are bears. I waited at the opening of my tent, with the campfire burning low. After a few minutes a rhythmic thumping, drumming sound began; the sound of someone banging a log against a tree trunk. Unmistakably, it was followed by very loud, high-pitched hoots and grunts.

I cannot be absolutely sure it was Sasquatch; I am sure that only those two things could be responsible for the noises heard.

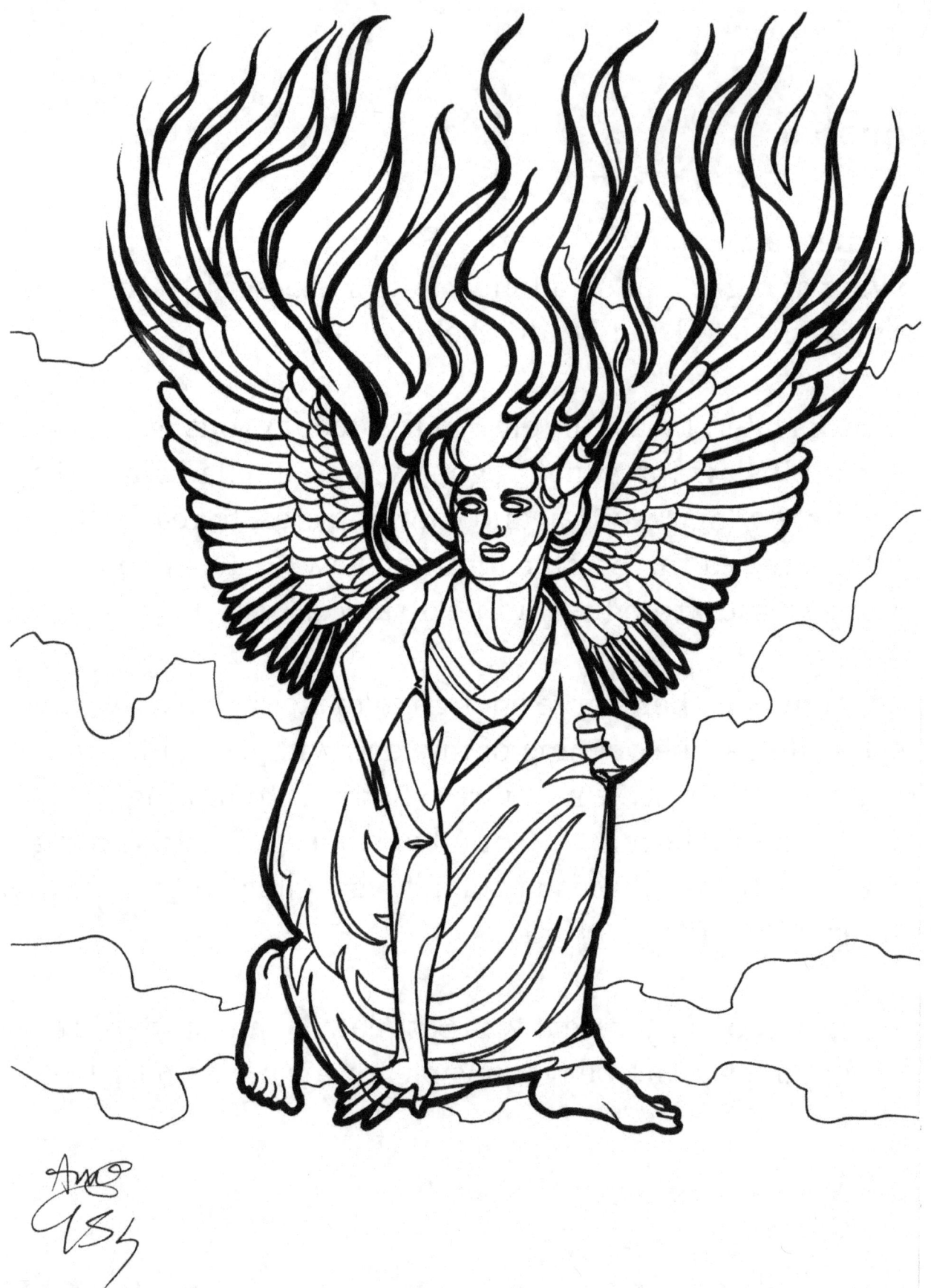

# Ifrit

Ifrits are from the Middle East. They're a type of djinn, yet an infernal sort. They're made of fire or smoke, and live underground or in ruined buildings or abandoned mosques. They're known for their cunning and trickery.

Ifrits can't be killed or defeated with any material weapons, only magic and superior trickery and cunning can defeat them.

They are prone to jealousy and may fall in love with a human, causing woe to all around that person. Only by causing them to make a promise can torture this be stopped, as they cannot go back on their word.

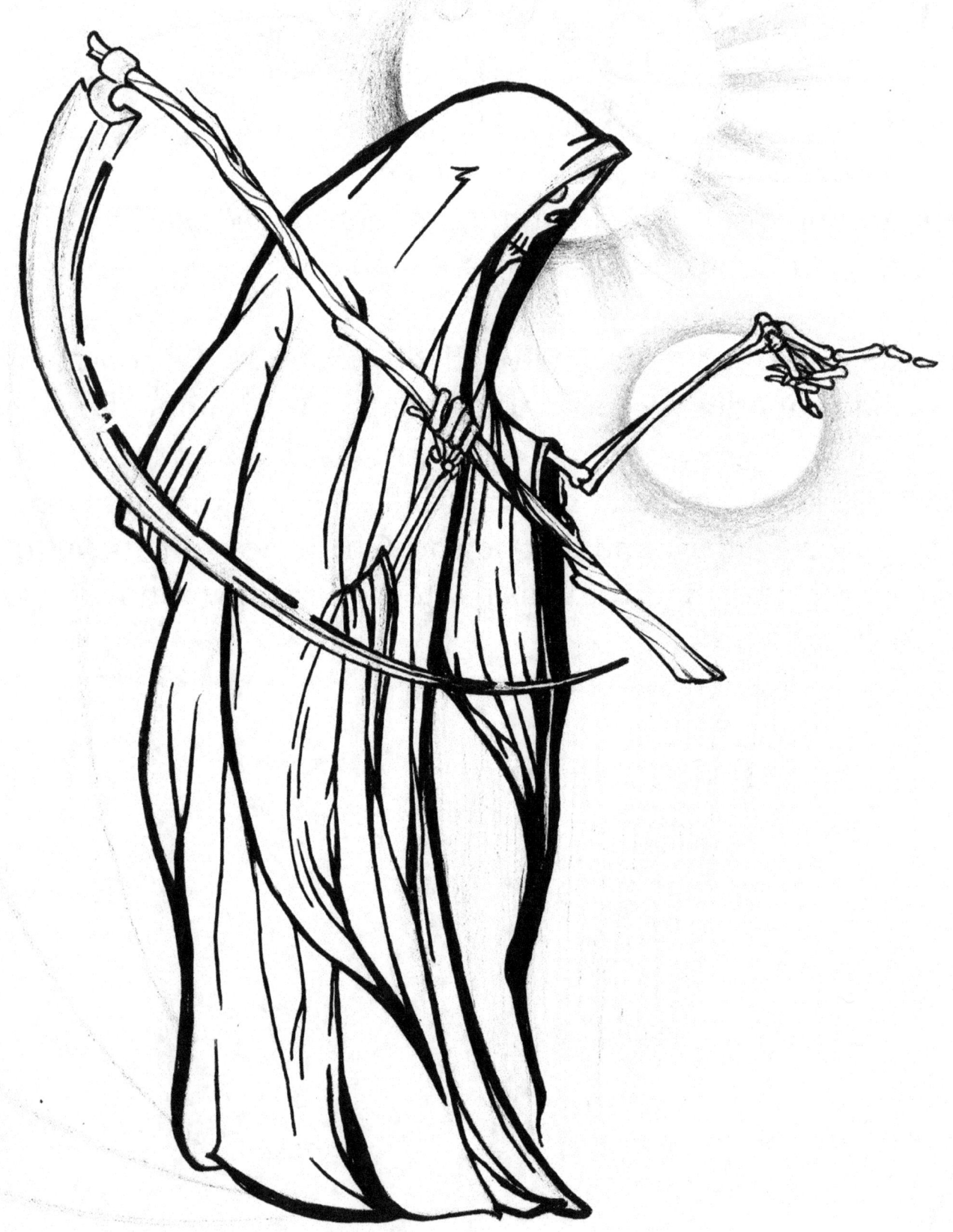

# Santa Muerte

Santa Muerte is a Mexican saint, but not recognized by the Catholic Church (or any other). She is said to represent death itself; she is often worshipped by people in dangerous or illegal occupations.

It is said that Santa Muerte can guarantee a peaceful death, which is the reason so many people make regular offerings to her. There are many shrines to this saint, found all over Central America and southern North America.

She holds a scythe, and sometimes an hourglass or a globe in her hands. Since she's not a recognized saint, she's a supernatural figure, one that millions of people fear and respect.

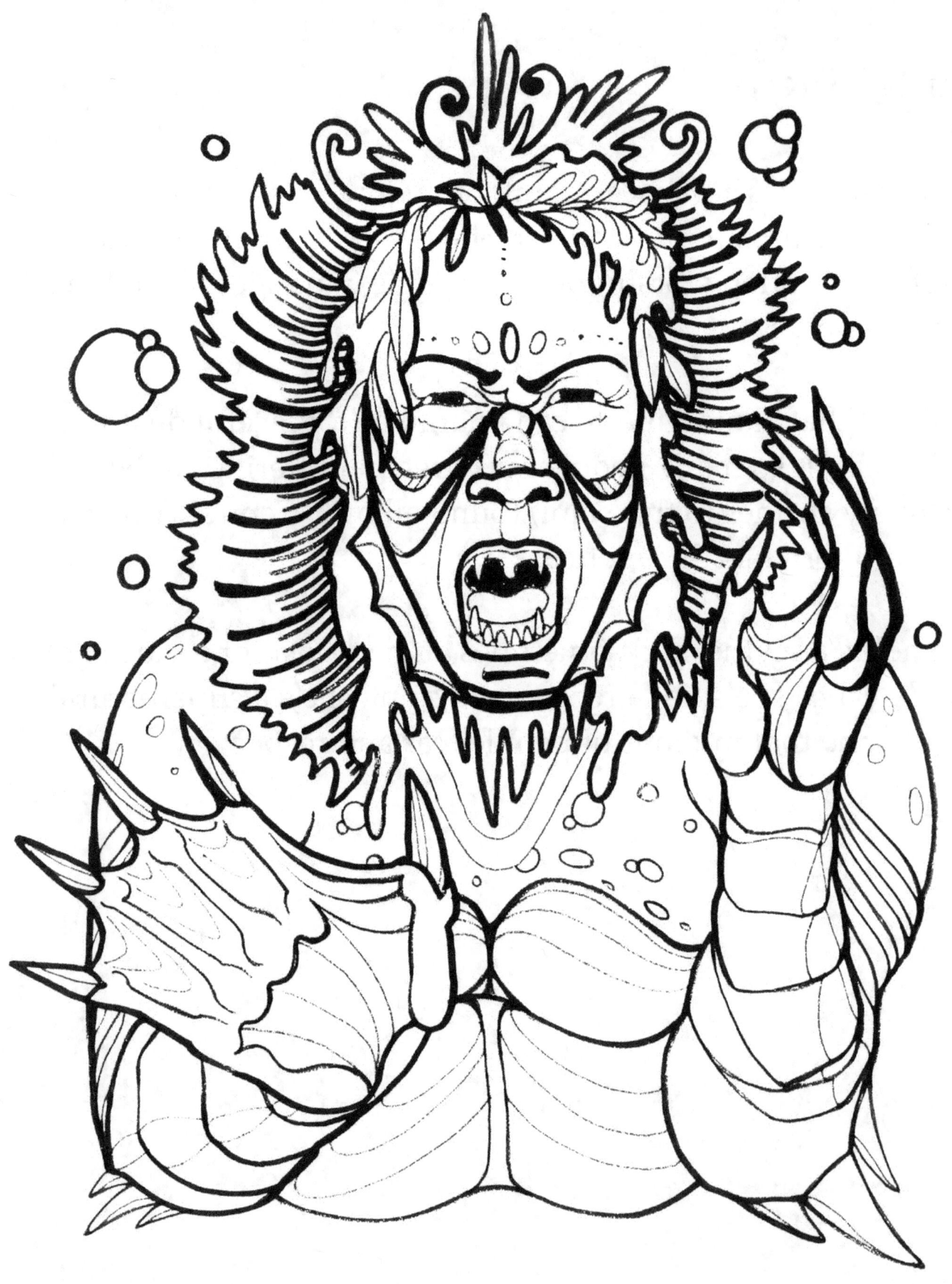

# Kaijin

The Kaijin is a legendary water creature from Japan. It's humanoid, and has webbing between its fingers and toes, with a large flap of skin around its waist.

They can only live out of water briefly, but are known to visit humans along the coast and lakes. Kaijin legends vary. Some are simply sighted, with no contact. Others have been said to carry off livestock and children.

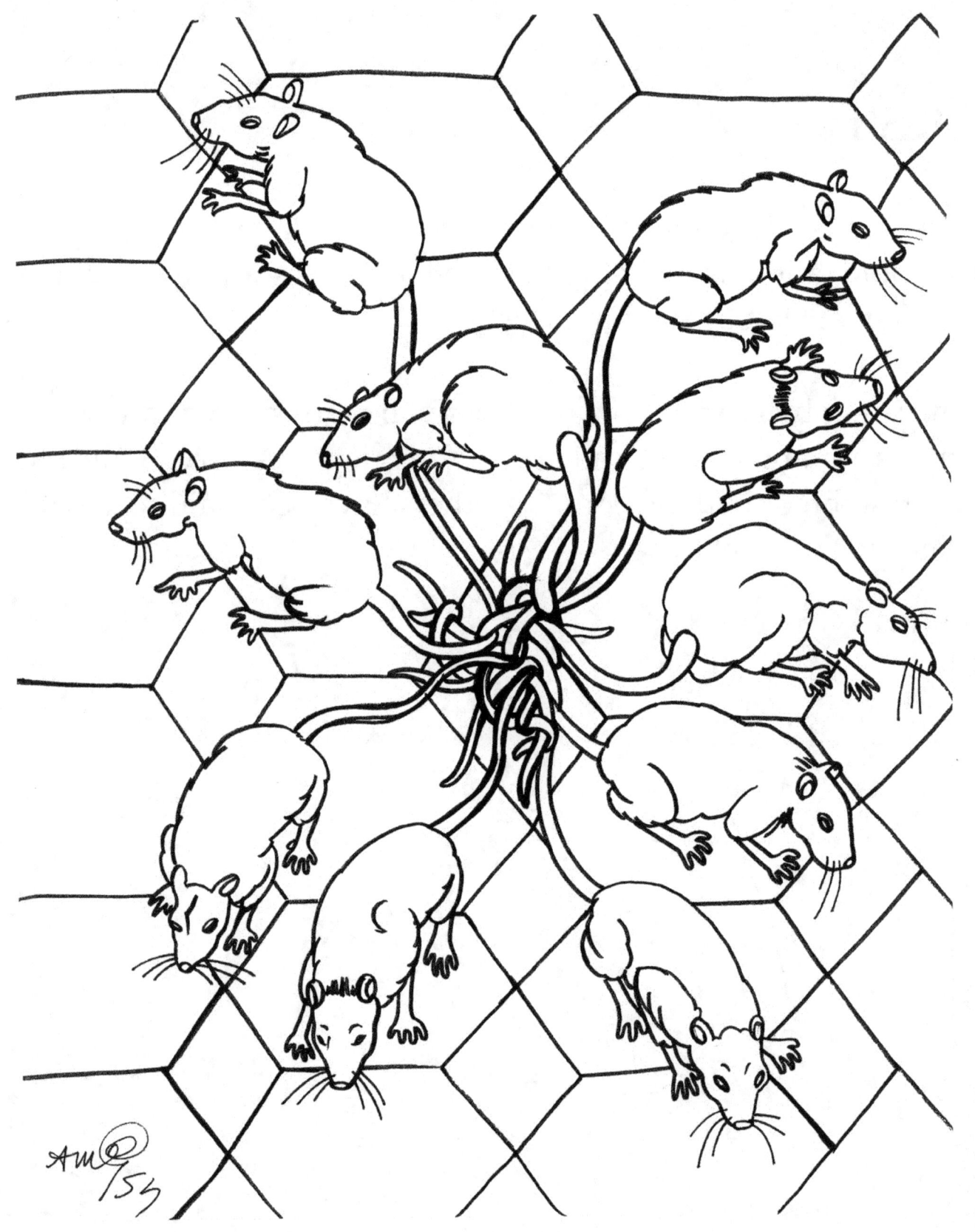

# Rat King

The Rat King is an old European myth. It is a group of living rats that have been tied together by the tail, knotted into one animal almost. They act in unison and are often found in abandoned mines and houses.

They're said to be a very bad omen, as Rat Kings were found before each epidemic of the plague, in various areas in Europe; and again before a bad epidemic of yellow fever there.

They are portents of doom on a large scale, predicting mass death rather than personal misfortune.

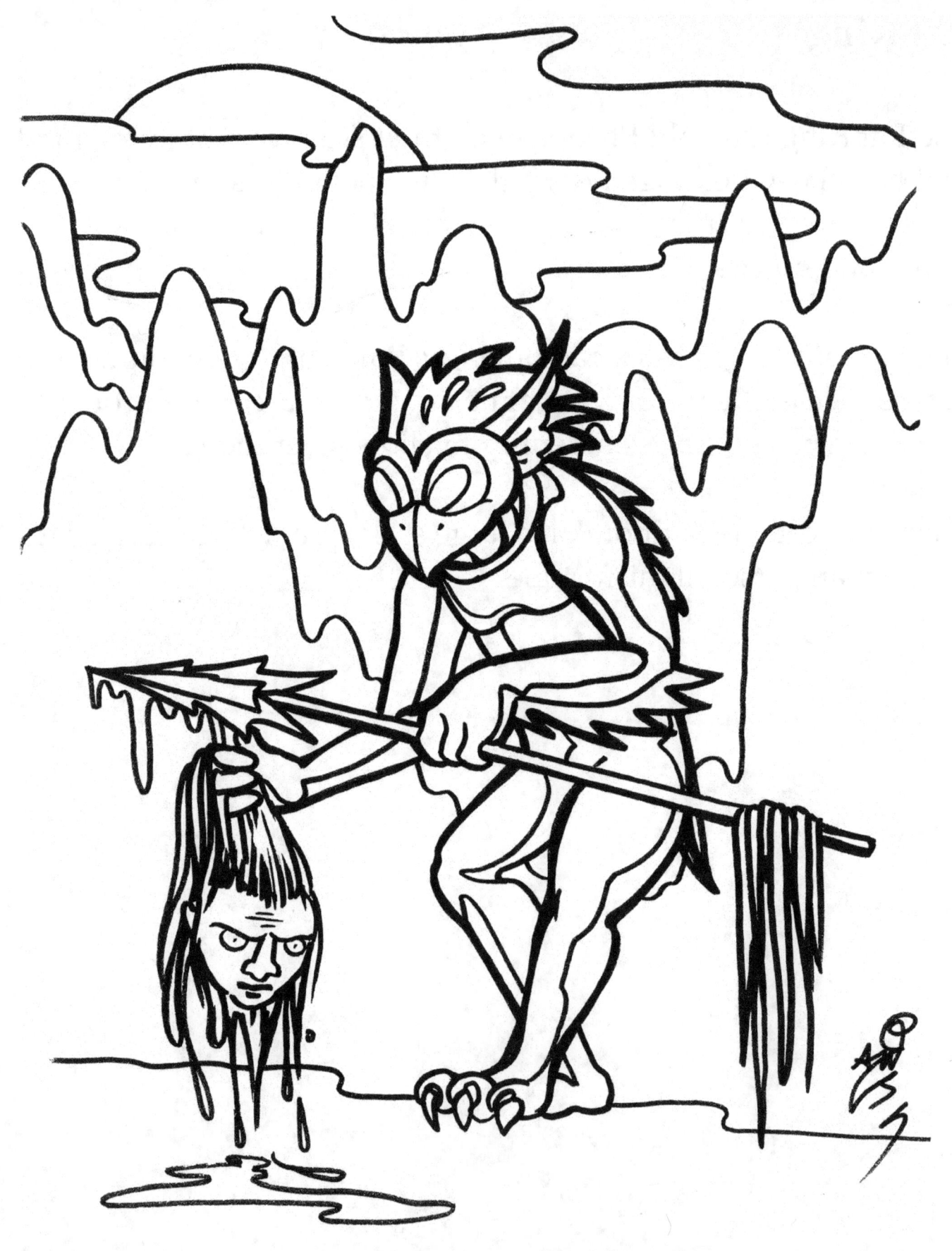

# Kappa

In China and Japan, Kappa are known as cryptids that inhabit ponds and rivers. They're tiny, as small as a child and sometimes mistaken for one.

They are reptilian in texture but have almost-human faces. There are different types of Kappas, some have an indentation in their head which they must keep full of water at all times (these can be destroyed by bowing at them, as when they bow back, their heads will empty and they die.)

Other Kappas are simply small humanoids who fish and swim in the rivers, living alongside humans like the Yeti or Sasquatch. Simply avoiding them if you see them is enough, as they're not aggressive unless provoked.

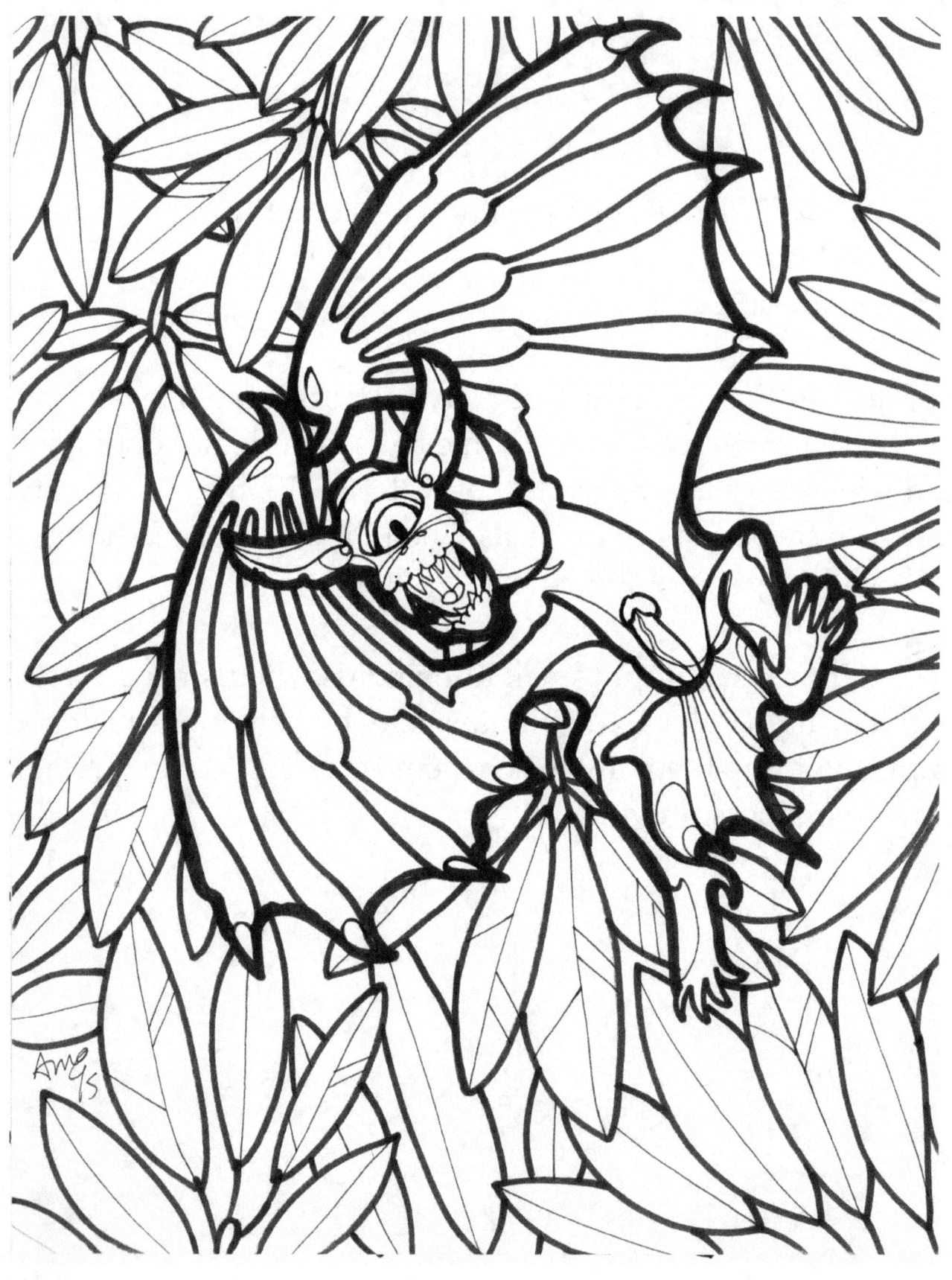

# Popobawa

The Popobawa is known in Tasmania as a type of incubus-like creature. It attacks virile men at night in their beds. It looks like an ordinary man by day, but at night it transforms into a bat-like creature, with immense wings and a gigantic penis.

It prefers to attack skeptical men, going as far to sodomize them. It may threaten a repeat attack unless the victim tells everyone about the Popobawa. The Popobawa becomes very angry if its existence is denied, sometimes attacking in retaliation.

Many men in the region sleep outdoors, on porches or hammocks, to avoid the Popobawa.

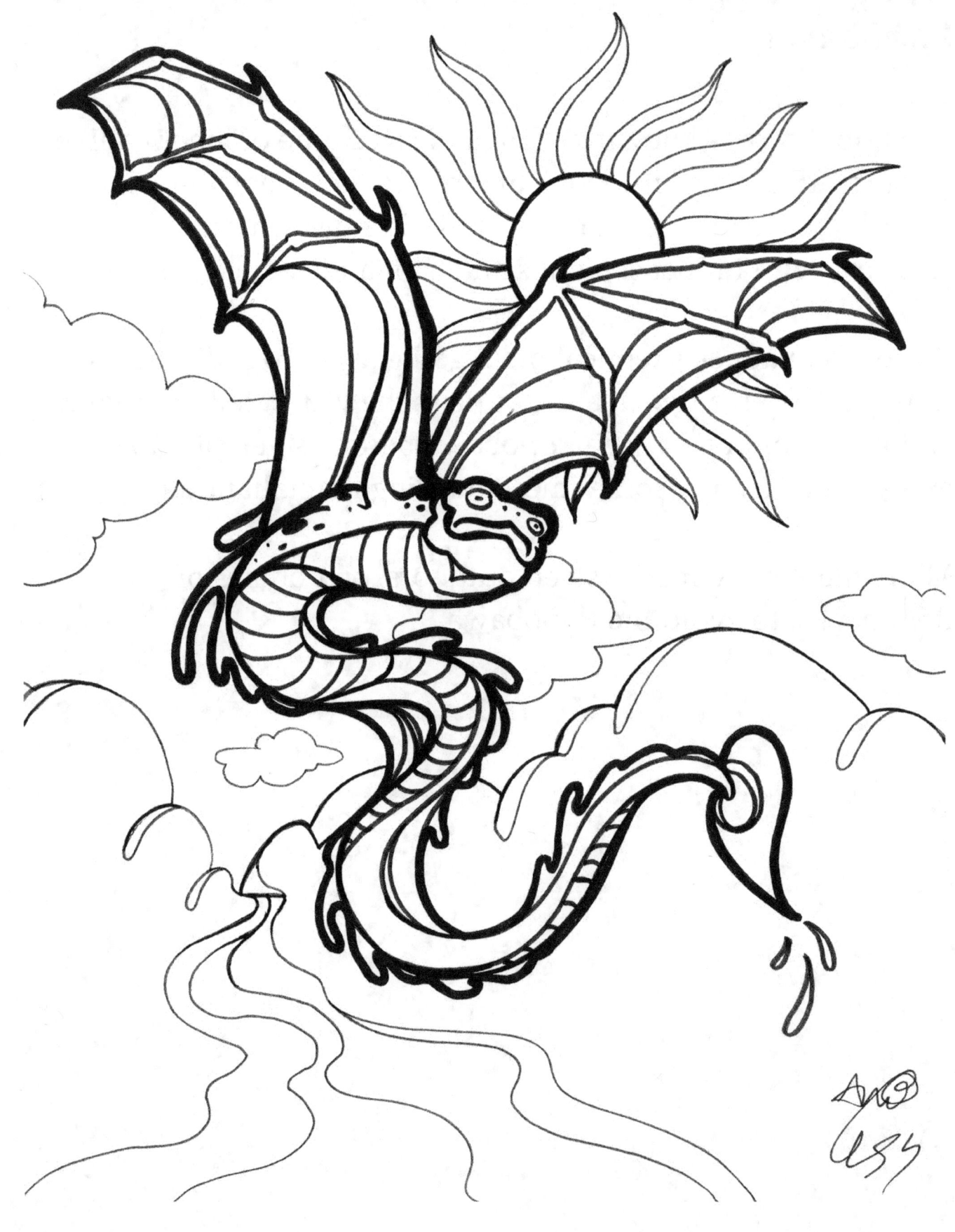

# Llamhigyn Y Dwr

The Llamhigyn Y Dwr is a welsh cryptid, originating in local folklore. It is a frog that can fly like a bat, and has a long tail with a stinger at the tip. It lives in bogs, lakes, ponds and rivers in Wales and will leap out and sting fishermen and others walking in the water where it lives.

It's also known as a trickster, snapping fishing nets and lines, eating livestock kept near water, attacking women who wash clothing in the river, and occasionally stinging then devouring a fisherman.

They tend to be most active at dusk and dawn, hence it's best to fish after sunrise, rather than in the wee hours of the morning.

Many night-fishers have reported being attacked by the Llamhigyn Y Dwr.

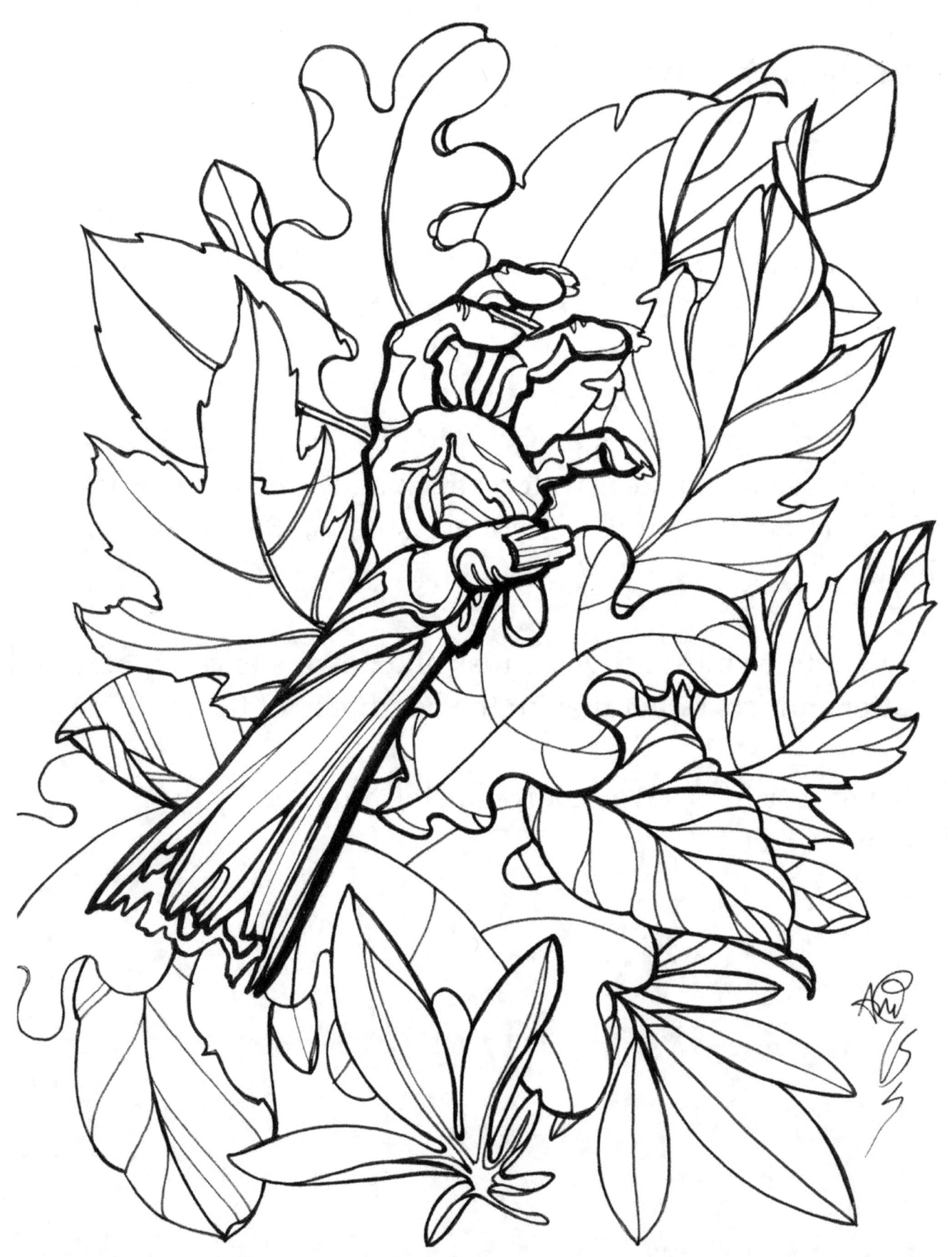

# Oniate

An Iroquois legend shares how a mummified hand can cause all manner of curses on the victim who touch it.

The Oniate is a dried hand which appears of its own accord, sometimes floating toward a victim. If it touches a person, it may cause blindness, unexplained illnesses, or result in death. It's sometimes called the ghost hand. It can be summoned by certain people, but more often simply appears, to punish those who behave badly.

It targets those who start arguments among family and friends, who get involved in other people's business, or who gossip.

Sometimes it appears if an elder is treated disrespectfully. It will appear out of thin air, and touch the person it wishes to curse.

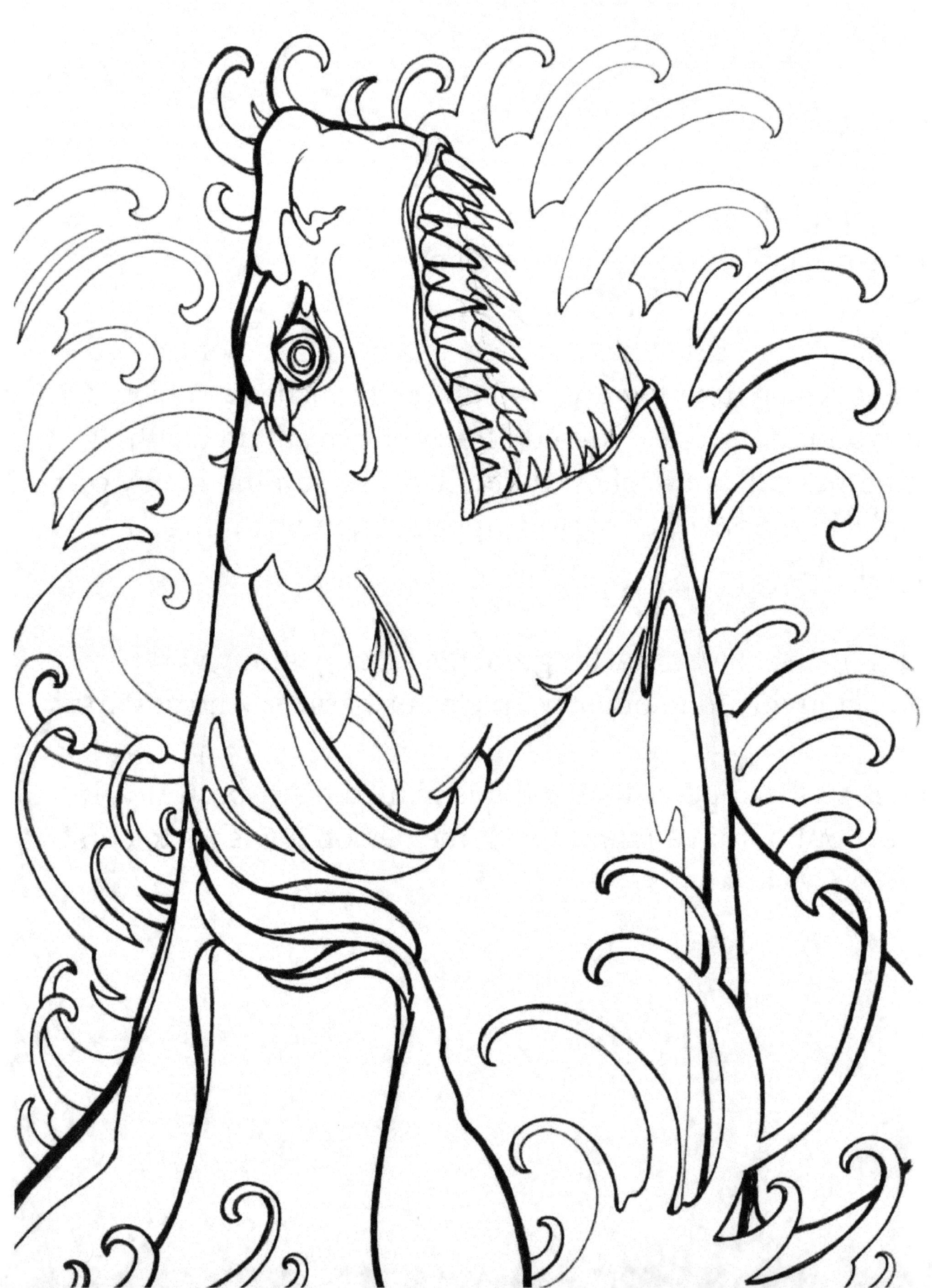

# Megalodon

This cryptid actually existed at one time. The last of these massive prehistoric animals died about two million years ago. There have been sightings, reports of attacks by them on other large sea animals; additionally many fictional stories filmed or written about them in the last few decades.

Some people claim that a small population could have survived in the deep ocean, and that they are still in existence. However it's unlikely.

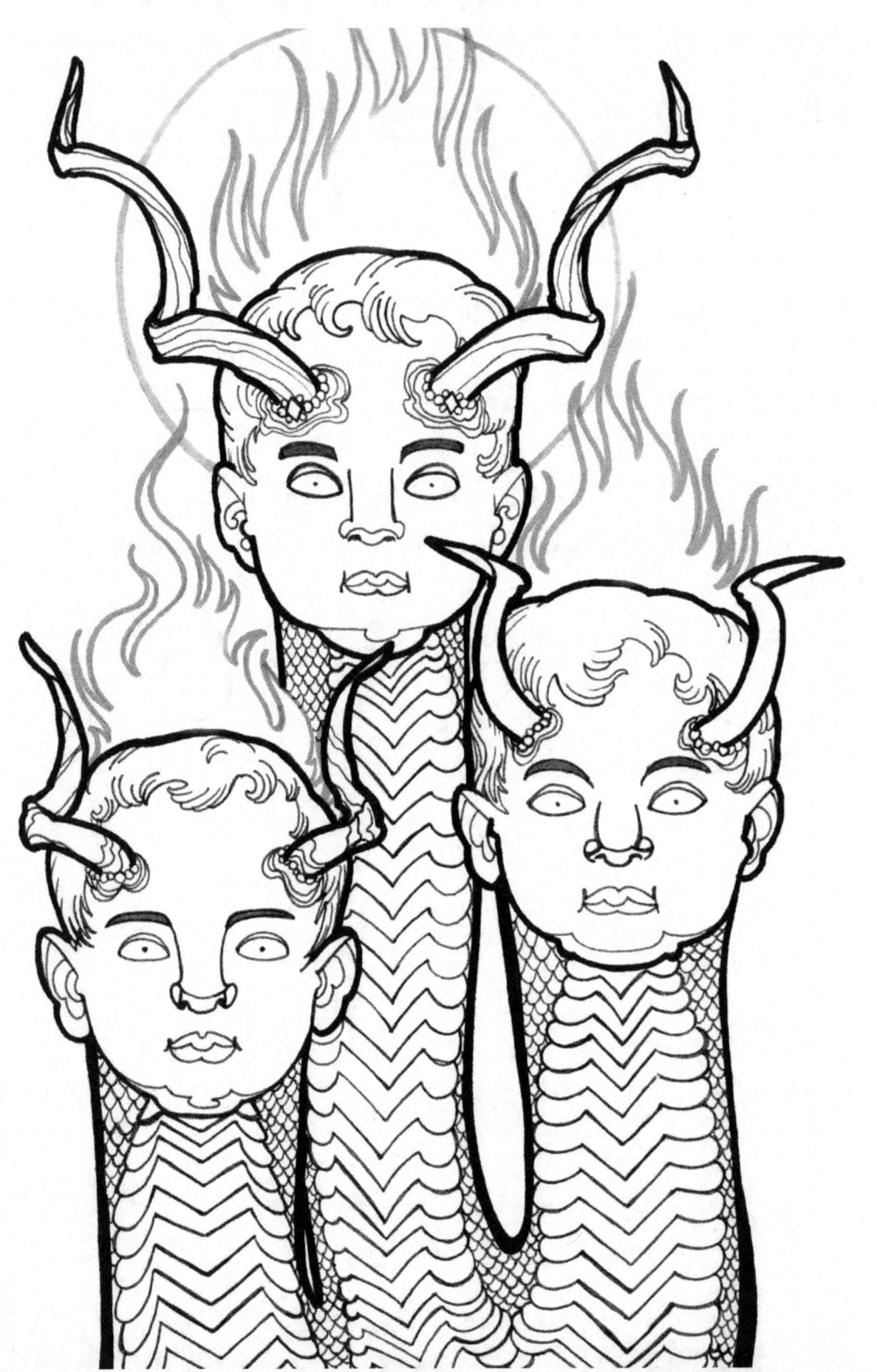

# Nagas

Nagas are of Hindu mythology. They're snake beings, with human heads and intelligence. Originally divine beings, folklore has changed their story into one of creatures to be feared.

They're considered to be guardians of springs, wells, and rivers. They cause both rain, and disasters like floods and drought. They become enraged by the mistreatment of the environment.

They live in the underground netherworld, and use anthills as their gate to this world. They retaliate with violence to any perceived mistreatment of the earth or of nature.

They are said to afflict people with skin disease, and cause natural calamities when retaliating.

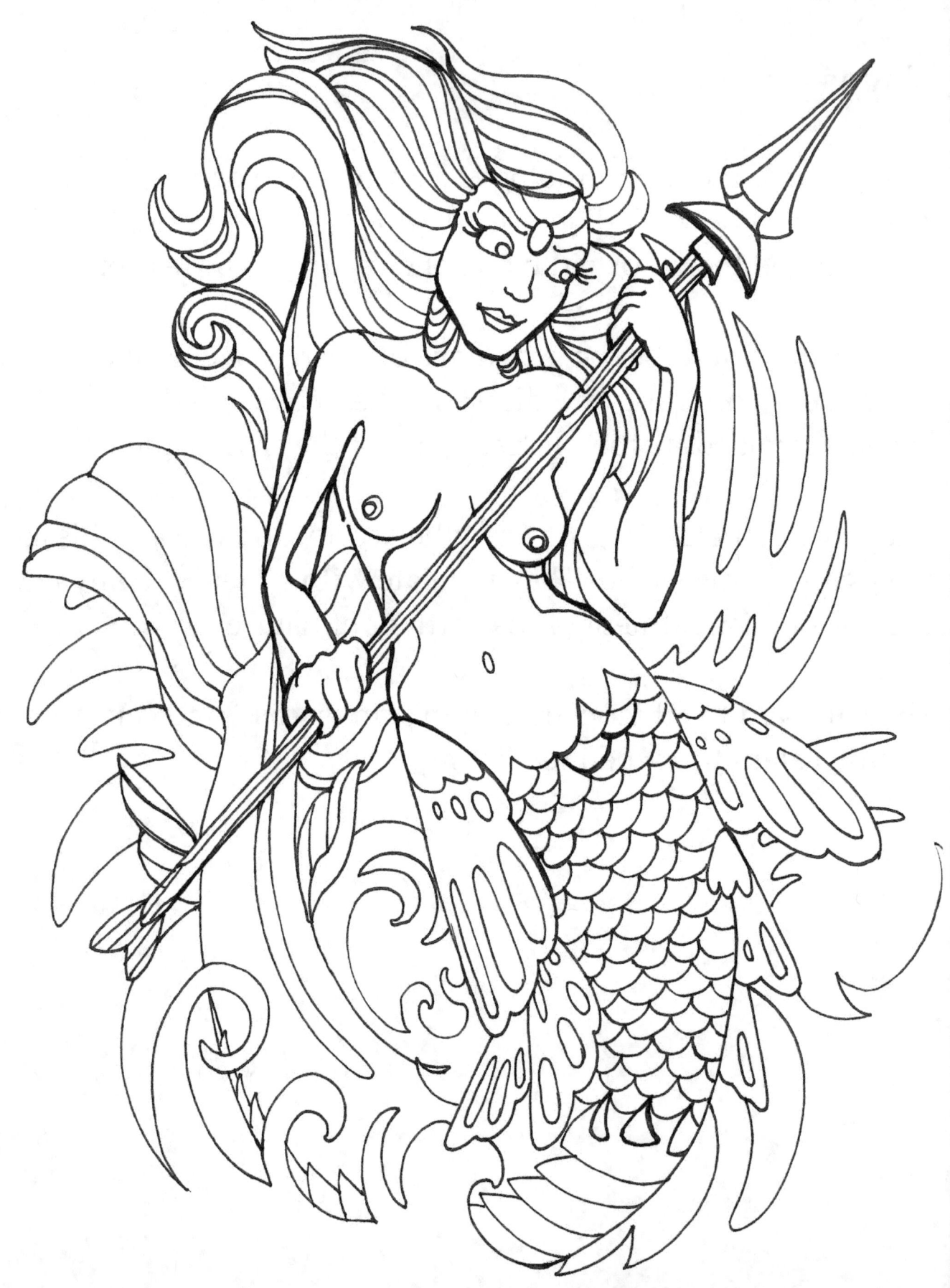

# Yacuruna or mermaid

The mermaid is reported worldwide. Mermen and mermaids seem to be common among folklore everywhere, though some cultures describe them as evil and wicked and others describe them as friendly and positive or lucky.

Fake documentaries aside, mermaids are usually sighted sunning themselves on rocks, drowning sailors, or fishing in the inlet of rivers near human habitations.

They seem to dislike humans in general and are rumored to drown sailors who might otherwise have survived a shipwreck.

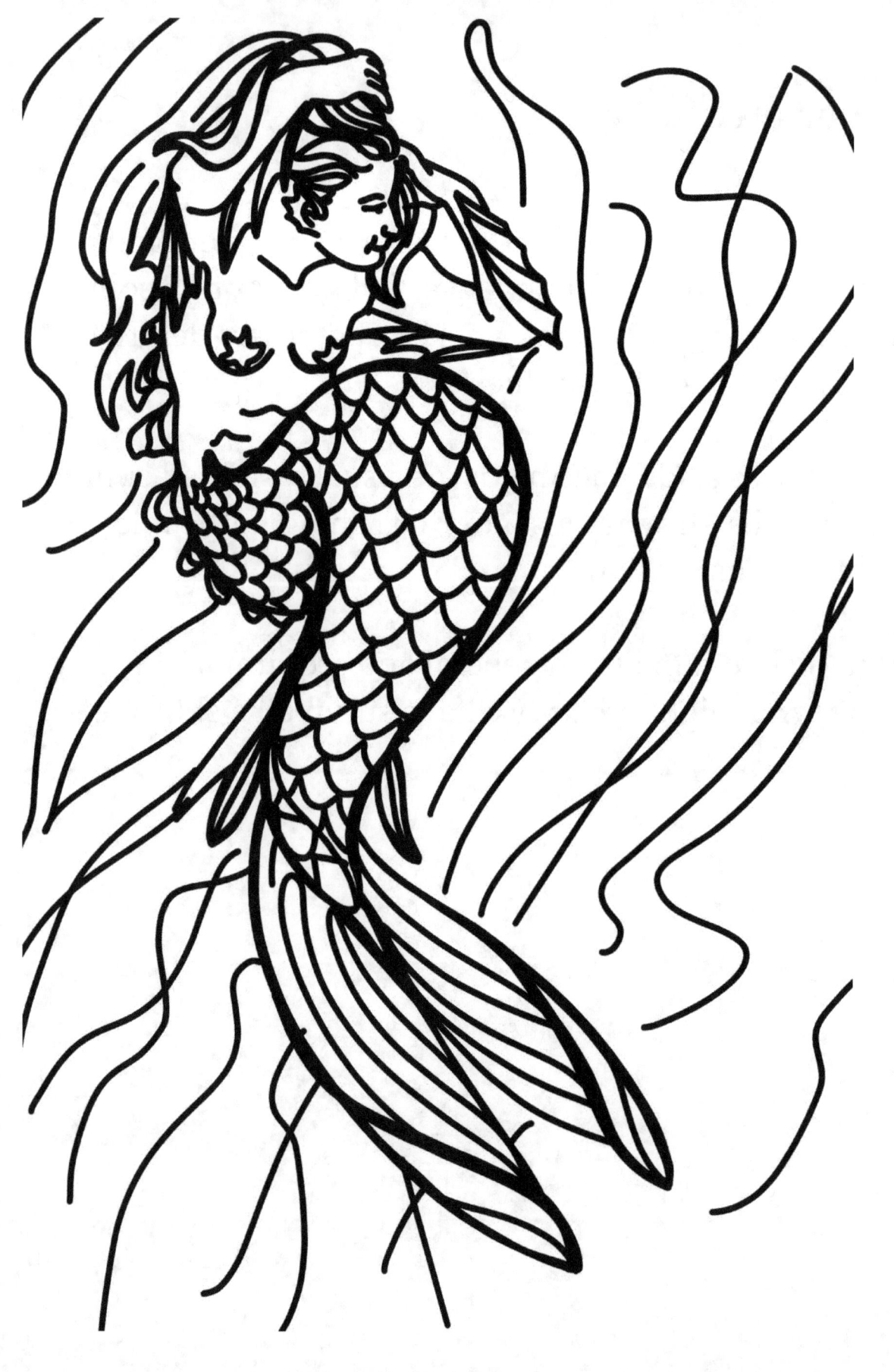

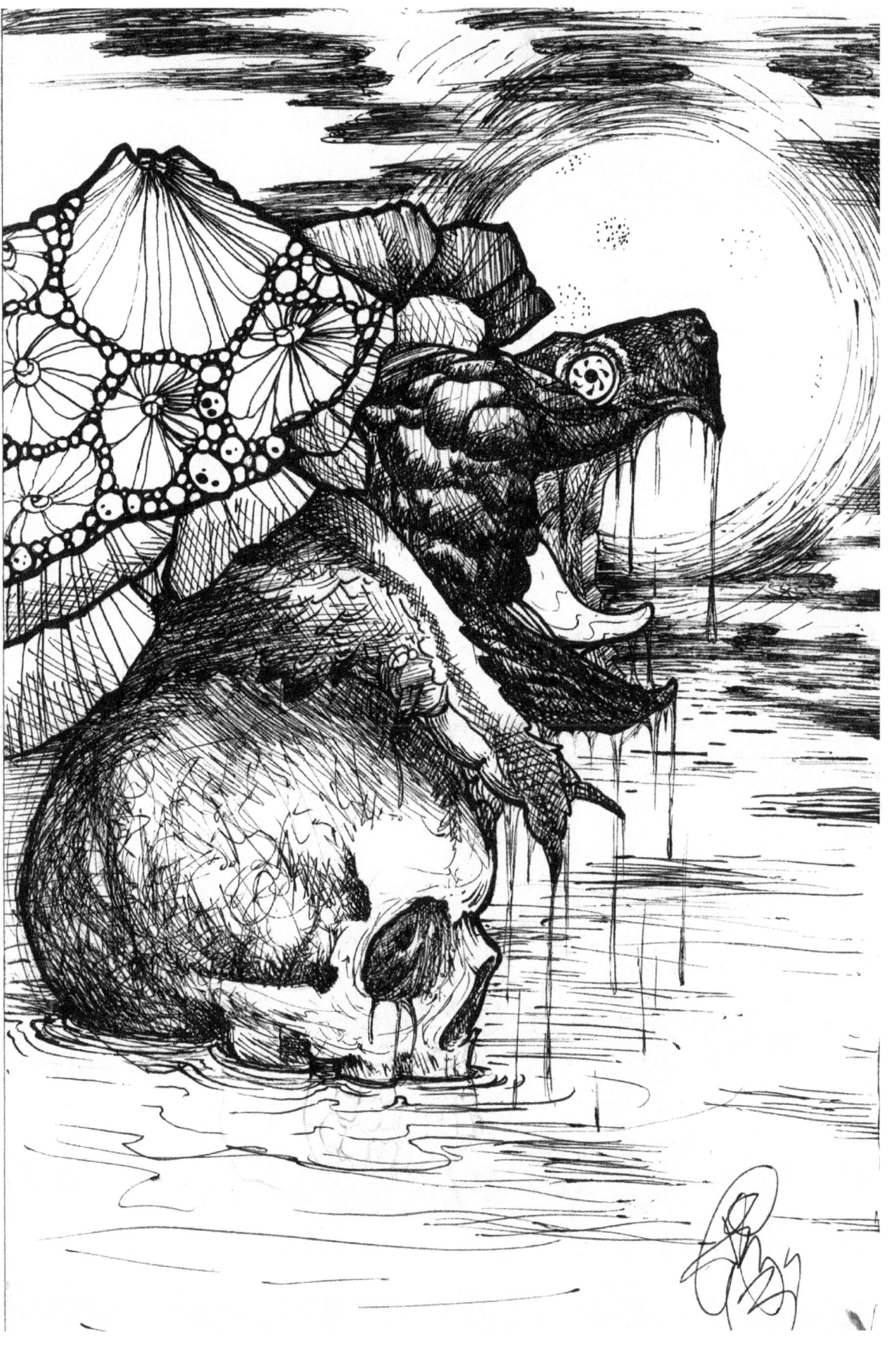

## About the Author

Anji Marth has been working in the arts since 1993. She is an internationally known, awarded tattoo artist, working professionally since 1999.

Anji learned to paint and draw from watching her uncle, David Borghi, whose work can be found in the Visionary Art Museum in Baltimore.

Marth's tattoos and art have been published in many tattoo-specific publications, including *Skin and Ink, Tattoo Magazine, Tattoo Flash Magazine, International Tattoo Art, Tattoo Veide* (German magazine), and *Outlaw Biker Tattoo Revue Magazine*. She's also been interviewed and featured in several of these magazines. She has also been interviewed and featured by Crime Library and truTV for her serial killer art series, and featured on *wired* online for her horror art.

Marth's writing has been published not only in tattoo magazines, but also in art magazines, local newspapers (*San Antonio, Sacramento, Seattle*), prose and poetry publications (*Gone Lawn, Emanations*), and horror zines.

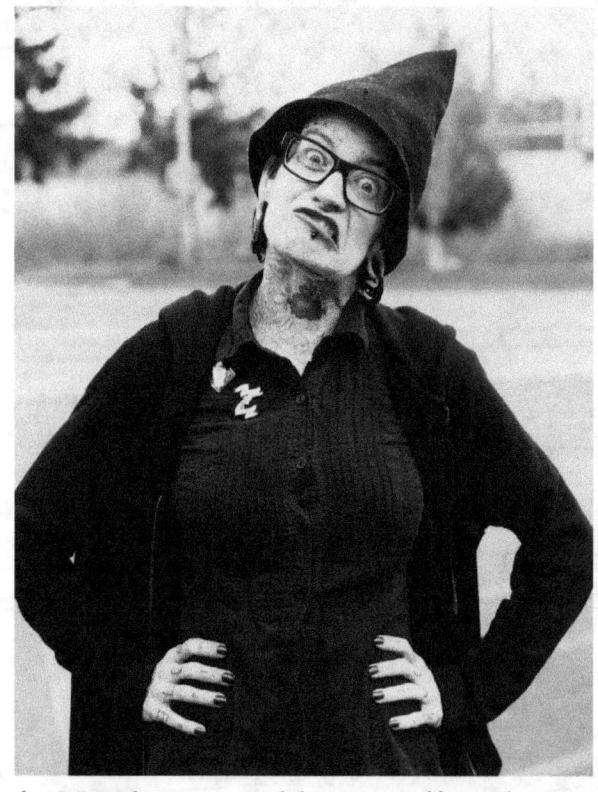

She lives in the Pacific Northwest and loves coffee, dogs, and interesting hats.
More of her work can be found via resonanteye.net

www.ingramcontent.com/pod-product-compliance
Lightning Source LLC
Chambersburg PA
CBHW062107220526
45471CB00010B/3642